EVERYDAY LIFE IN
ROMAN TIMES

The EVERYDAY LIFE series is one of the
best known and most respected of all
historical works, giving detailed insight into
the background life of a particular period.
This edition provides an invaluable and
vivid picture of everyday life in Roman
times from the Claudian Conquest of
Britain in A.D. 43 to the fall of the
Roman Empire.

The *New Statesman* has commended the
Quennells' 'rare gift for arousing historical
imagination', and this volume is an
outstanding account of how ordinary
people lived during the great changes
in everyday life caused by the Roman
Occupation.

Other EVERYDAY LIFE books

published by Carousel Books

Marjorie and C. H. B. Quennell

EVERYDAY LIFE IN
ROMAN TIMES

Carousel Editor: Anne Wood

TRANSWORLD PUBLISHERS LTD
A National General Company

EVERYDAY LIFE IN ROMAN TIMES

A CAROUSEL BOOK 0 552 54014 5

Originally published in Great Britain
by B. T. Batsford Ltd. as *Everyday Life in Roman Britain*

PRINTING HISTORY
Batsford edition published 1924
Batsford revised edition published 1959
Carousel edition published 1972

Carousel books are published by Transworld
Publishers Ltd.,
Cavendish House, 57–59 Uxbridge Road,
Ealing, London, W.5.

Made and printed in Great Britain by
Cox & Wyman Ltd., London, Reading and Fakenham

PREFACE

THE BOYS and girls for whom we write, may have read the *Life of Agricola*, by Tacitus, and so know the fine Epilogue with which it closes.

'And I would lay this charge on his daughter and his wife – so to reverence the memory of their father, and husband, that they revolve within them all that he said and did, and to cherish the form and the fashion of his soul, rather than of his body; it is not that I would forbid the making of statues, shaped in marble or bronze, but that as the human face, so is its copy – futile and perishing, while the form of the mind is eternal, to be expressed, not through the alien medium of art and its material, but severally by each man in the fashion of his own life.'

Tacitus was writing of the character of his father-in-law, Agricola, and gave us at the same time a hint of what we should look for in history. If only the spirit is eternal, it is very obvious that we must make diligent search for the principles which have animated men in the past and helped them to fashion their souls. To search for motive is apt to be an arid study; political history, and its recital of how statesmen have bested their friends, and ruined their enemies, makes dull reading, unless it is inspired. There remains the possibility of judging men by their works. This was the only method in the Prehistoric periods, and it is on the whole a very safe one.

In dealing with Roman history we shall find the historians divided into two schools, one of which will glorify the Republic and think the Empire was all decline and fall; the other will thrill at the Augustan Age. It is safe to predict, that to whichever school we attach ourselves, or even if we form an opinion of our own, we shall leave off with a feeling of great respect for the Roman sense of law and order.

When a nation not only makes laws, but agrees to keep them, it is a sign of a very advanced state of civilization. With this Roman power of administration, we shall note great developments in the art of town-planning, building, and civil engineering. Yet all this wonderful structure came tumbling down, because the fashion of the Roman soul was too material.

The period dealt with in this book is vital to us because the introduction of Christianity into Great Britain dates from the Roman Occupation, and conflicted in a thousand ways with the Roman conception of life and living.

The Roman was tolerant. Caesar writing of the gods of the Gauls, said they were much the same as other peoples, and the Romans, as a proud and conquering race, were not alarmed at the preaching of the disciples of an obscure Jew who had been crucified in Palestine. They persecuted the Christians, not so much for saying that man was made in the image of God, but for political rather than for religious reasons. It is almost impossible for us, with centuries of Christian teaching behind us, to estimate the first effect of the teaching of the Apostles. We know the teaching, even if we neglect it, but to have heard the Sermon on the Mount, as a Roman, for the first time, must have been an extraordinary experience. If he believed the teaching, then his confidence as a Roman was gone, because Christianity was the negation of the Roman way of living, and contributed to its downfall.

Ambrose, Bishop of Milan, made Theodosius the Emperor, in A.D. 390, divest himself of the purple and do public penance for a massacre carried out by his troops. Power had passed to the Church.

In the wide region of Statecraft, we can watch the efforts of man to govern himself. Hill forts could only have been formed under some system of tribal government, and in the historic period, we find Kings and Empires, Tyrannies, Democracies, and Republics, tried one after the other, in man's search for the proper method of living.

From the time of the Roman Occupation, so far as Europe was concerned, Christianity was destined to become the great force by which men set the "fashion of their souls"; it civilized men again after the dark ages following on the fall of Rome, and inspired the Crusades. Churches were planned to be cruciform, and the figure of Christ was cut in stone, and glowed in the jewelled glass of a thousand windows.

It follows, then, that we are in sympathy with all the people, who, since A.D. was used in the calendar, have been confronted with similar problems of life and death, of joy and sorrow, and of how life is to be made sweet and wholesome.

The statesman reads history to find how man can be helped to this end, and his trouble is the same as ours, how to make the dry bones live. There are times of enlightenment.

Our readers will sometimes have seen visions, and dreamed dreams. There are days, or better still nights, when the tired body is sloughed off, and the brain rides untrammelled, and we understand the meaning of things. The time curtains roll back a little on one side, and we have a walking part in the scene; we may not speak to the principal actors, but we are close to them; we catch the fragrance of Wolsey's orange as he passes along, and the figures of history become instead of names, men and women of flesh and blood.

We begin to form certain opinions of our own; one period may seem brave and cheerful, another dark and gloomy. For this reason, perhaps, history has been very much concerned with the doings of great men; even the terrible villains serve the useful purpose of shadow in the picture, and throw into relief the brightness of the heroes. If these have been rather dispensers of Death, than saviours of life, like Pasteur, then it is our own fault for having worshipped at the wrong shrine. This question of the atmosphere of history is worth testing by our own experience; this may be limited, but we can try to find out why a particular school, or form, or term, or individual, will leave an impression on our minds. The importance of history, or tradition, is that it gives us a standard against which we can measure our own effort, and as history is concerned just as much with work as war, so work is concerned with the doings of untold myriads of individuals much the same as ourselves.

MARJORIE AND C. H. B. QUENNELL

CONTENTS

LIST OF ILLUSTRATIONS

BIBLIOGRAPHY

Boumphrey, G. M., *Along the Roman Roads* (1935).

Caesar, *The Conquest of Gaul* (Penguin Books, 1951).

Charlesworth, M. P., *The Lost Province* (Cardiff, 1949).

Collingwood, R. G., *The Archaeology of Roman Britain* (Methuen, 1930).

Collingwood, R. G. and Myers, J. N. L., *Roman Britain and the English Settlements* (Oxford, 1945).

Curle, J., *A Roman Frontier Post: Newstead* (1911).

Margary, I. D., *Roman Roads in Britain* (Phoenix House, Vol I, 1955; Vol II, 1957).

Haverfield, F., *The Romanization of Roman Britain* (Oxford, 1923).

Haverfield, F., and Macdonald, G., *The Roman Occupation of Britain* (Oxford, 1924).

Macdonald, G., *The Roman Wall in Scotland* (Oxford, 1934).

Moore, R. W., *The Romans in Britain*. A selection of Latin Texts (Methuen, 1938).

Richmond, Ian, *Roman Britain* (Collins, 1947).

Richmond, Ian, *Roman Britain* (Penguin Books, 1955).

Rivet, A. L. F., *Town and Country in Roman Britain* (Hutchinson 1957).

Tacitus: *On Great Britain and Germany* (Penguin Books, 1948).

Ordnance Survey, *Map of Roman Britain*. With very good Lists and Introduction (3rd edition, 1956).

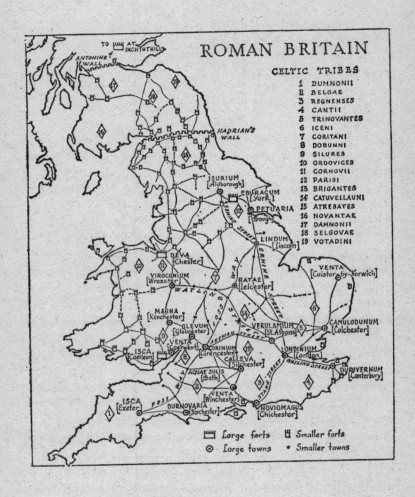

ROMAN BRITAIN

CELTIC TRIBES

1 DUMNONII
2 BELGAE
3 REGNENSES
4 CANTII
5 TRINOVANTES
6 ICENI
7 CORITANI
8 DOBUNNI
9 SILURES
10 ORDOVICES
11 CORNOVII
12 PARISI
13 BRIGANTES
14 CATUVELLAUNI
15 ATREBATES
16 NOVANTAE
17 DAMNONII
18 SELGOVAE
19 VOTADINI

TO AT INCHTUTHILL

ANTONINE WALL

HADRIAN'S WALL

ISURIUM [Aldborough]
EBURACUM [York]
PETUARIA [Brough]
DEVA [Chester]
VIROCONIUM [Wroxeter]
LINDUM [Lincoln]
RATAE [Leicester]
VENTA [Caistor-by-Norwich]
MAGNA [Kenchester]
GLEVUM [Gloucester]
VERULAMIUM [St.Albans]
CAMULODUNUM [Colchester]
VENTA [Caerwent]
CORINIUM [Cirencester]
ISCA [Caerleon]
CALLEVA [Silchester]
LONDINIUM [London]
AQUAE SULIS [Bath]
DUROVERNUM [Canterbury]
ISCA [Exeter]
VENTA [Winchester]
DURNOVARIA [Dorchester]
NOVIOMAGUS [Chichester]

ERMINE STREET
WATLING STREET
FOSS WAY
AKEMAN STREET
STANE STREET
WATLING STREET

⌂ Large forts   ⌂ Smaller forts
◉ Large towns   • Smaller towns

THE HERITAGE OF ROME

THE Roman occupation was one of the most interesting periods in our history, in which the greatest
changes were to be effected in our everyday life. For
some 367 years, Britain, which was not yet England,
was to form part of an Empire which stretched from
Babylon, around both sides of the Mediterranean, and
up through France to our country. We were to be
quite suddenly familiarized with the best which the
older European civilization had to offer in the way of
Science and Art; and all this wealth of ideas was to be
thrust on us when we had not advanced much beyond
the stage of being turbulent tribesmen.

Let us look back a little and find out what the
Britons were like before the Claudian Conquest of
A.D. 43. In *Everyday Life in Prehistoric Times* we finished
up with the Glastonbury Lake Village. Here, on a low
island in the marshes the inhabitants built wattle
and daub huts with thatched roofs, and surrounded
these with a stockaded fence. The general appearance
must have been that of an East African village today.
It had no shape or town-plan; the huts were not set
out in any regular arrangement. The whole layout was
higgledy-piggledy and haphazard. The people were
good craftsmen – could smelt and forge iron, weave,
turn wood, and make pottery. The Glastonbury
Lake villagers and the inhabitants of other villages all

over England, were farmers, able to supply themselves
with food and clothing without outside help. But
they were not very well organized or very strong and
they were always in danger from bands of marauders.

The mere fact of building the Glastonbury Lake
Village in a swamp shows that the people must have
been afraid, and disaster fell upon them some little
time before the Roman occupation. Perhaps they were
attacked by the Belgic invaders, who began to arrive
in England about 200 B.C., and who seem to have been
better organized and equipped with superior weapons
of war. But even these Belgic tribes and the other
Celtic inhabitants of Britain at the time of the Roman
invasion were only small groups of farmers under
warlike chieftains. They had in fact fled into England
to get out of the way of the Romans who had occupied
Gaul (France and part of Germany) a century
before, or to avoid other superior tribes of barbarians
warring along the frontiers of Civilization. Britain
at this time can be compared with the Wild West of
America a century ago, when the motto was 'go west,
young man' and carve out a kingdom for yourself in
No Man's Land.

Now think of the feelings of the early Britons as
towns like Silchester (Fig. 6) began to arise in the
first century A.D. It must have been an extraordinary
experience for them to have watched one of the
Roman surveyors at work, and noticed how carefully
he set out the town – that it was in fact town-planned;
or to see its Basilica (Fig. 24), with its Corinthian
order of architecture, rising from the ground. Or to
go to Bath and see the great bathing establishment
there, with its lead-lined baths, and intricate plumbing
and heating work. The Britons must have heard of the

doings of the Romans in Gaul, but probably, like the Queen of Sheba, had not believed, and then when they were confronted with their work, there must have been 'no more spirit' in them.

Or take the roads. The two-wheeled chariots of the Britons probably kept to the high ground, and used the trackways which had come down to them from Neolithic times. The lowlands would have been too swampy. Now think of the Roman roads which we still use. We construct laboriously a few miles of arterial roads, or make a by-pass – the Romans covered their Empire with roads which all led to Rome.

Little can be known of the literature of the Britons; doubtless some Homer sang their tribal lays and tales, but no one wrote them down. Nevertheless, their Celtic myths and legends were handed down, and becoming traditional did, in the Middle Ages, develop into a literature peculiarly our own. Against this it must be remembered that the men who arrived here in A.D. 43 were familiar with the masterpieces of Greek and Roman literature. Cicero died in 43 B.C.; Virgil was born in 70 B.C.; and Horace published his Odes in 23 B.C. So the Latin tongue, which was to become a universal language, had already taken form to itself, and was to be heard in our country wherever the Romans came together.

Sir Mortimer Wheeler excavated parts of the Roman city of Verulamium (St. Albans) before the war and this work is being continued year by year as a training school for London University students. Many exciting discoveries have been made in recent years. Here we are concerned with the excavation of the Roman theatre of Verulamium – the only one of its kind in Britain. We hope all our readers will visit this theatre, and it may be as well, before so doing, to study the lie of the land on a map. The Roman Watling Street ran straight through the Roman Verulamium, on its way from St. Stephens, to the south of St. Albans, on to Redbourn, and part of it is now the entrance drive to Gorhambury. So it will be well to steer for St. Michael's Church, about half a mile to the west of St. Albans. Here we shall be in the middle of the old Roman city, in fact, the vicarage of the church is built on the site of its forum, and close by is the theatre.

Fig. 2 shows a reconstruction of the theatre when first built about A.D. 140; it must be taken with a grain of salt. The plan at the side shows the central orchestra about 80 feet in diameter, and surrounded by a wall. The outer wall, with buttresses, formed the retaining walls for the earth banks, made by sinking the orchestra below the general level. The people sat on wooden seats on the earth banks, and these were reached from external stairs. There were passages down to the orchestra from the outside, and over two of these may have been seats for the notables. The stage occupied only about 48 feet of the perimeter of the orchestra, and behind it was the dressing-room for the actors.

The first thing to be remembered is that this is the only Roman theatre in Britain; and second, that it is more Greek than Roman in plan. Miss Kenyon, however, who has written a very good handbook which can be bought on the site, points out that similar theatres were built in Gaul. All theatres date back to the circular threshing floors, on which the ancient Greeks danced in honour of Dionysus, the god of the vine and fertility, when he had given them a

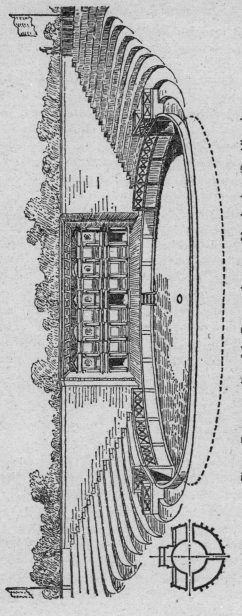

Fig. 2 Reconstruction of the Roman theatre at Verulamium (St. Albans)

good harvest – that is why the central space is called
the orchestra, because it comes from the Greek word
to dance.

In the sixth and fifth centuries B.C. the Greeks began
to produce plays, and so a stage was introduced for the
actors. The Romans ordinarily cut the orchestra in
half so that it was a semi-circle and much more like a
modern theatre. Why did they revert to the Greek
type in Britain? Again why did they put a wall
round the orchestra at Verulamium? We think that it
was because the theatre there was not only used for
dances and spectacles, but possible bear-baiting.
The orchestra, in fact, was on its way to be turned into
the pit. However that may be, go and see the excavations. Another good little book by Mr. Lowther can be
bought there, showing the later alterations. Then
sadly enough in the fourth century A.D. Britain became
so unsettled that there was no time for plays, or even
bear-baiting, and the theatre became the midden for
the rubbish of a dwindled town.

When we come to the beliefs of the Britons we have
more to go on. Caesar wrote, in the Gallic Wars, of
the Druidism which was the religion of the later
Celtic tribes of Britain and Gaul:

The whole Gaulish nation is to a great degree
devoted to superstitious rites; and on this account
those who are afflicted with severe diseases, or who
are engaged in battles and dangers, either sacrifice
human beings for victims, or vow that they will
immolate themselves. These employ the Druids as
ministers for such sacrifices, because they think
that, unless the life of man be repaid for the life of
man, the will of the immortal gods cannot be

appeased. Others make wicker-work images of vast size, the limbs of which they fill with living images and set on fire.

It is a common error to associate the Druids with Stonehenge, but this had been built nearly 2000 years before. The Romans were tolerant of the beliefs of those whom they conquered, but Druidism seems to have shocked even the Romans, until they finally destroyed it in its headquarters at Anglesey.

What makes our period for ever memorable is that the Roman occupation began soon after the birth of Our Lord. Christ was born in Palestine, and here it was, and in Asia Minor, that the greater part of the work of the Apostles was carried out. It is the tradition at Glastonbury that Joseph of Arimathea came there about A.D. 47, bringing with him a cup in which he had caught the last drops of Christ's blood, and this having been lost, the search for the Holy Grail became the great work of Arthur and his knights.

There must have been Christian legionaries, and in any case, after the Edict of Toleration in 313, they were free to worship in their own way. Figs. 13–15 illustrate the probable Christian Church at Silchester. From the blazing wicker images of the Druids to the Sermon on the Mount, preached at Silchester, is a revolutionary happening of prime importance to a Christian people.

In this period, then, our people were subjected to the three great civilizing influences in European civilization – the teaching of Greece, Rome, and Christianity.

There is an amusing idea that the Romans arrived here in A.D. 43, and departed in A.D. 410, during which time, 367 years, they kept themselves to themselves. That is equal to a period from the early days of Elizabeth's reign to 1937. Unless the legionary was quite unlike all other soldiers, it is probable that many of them fell in love with and married British maidens; so some of us, if we did but know, may have had Roman forbears. We know one Scotsman whose profile we have seen on Roman coins, and of course the Roman legionaries were recruited from all corners of the Empire – from the plains of Hungary and North Germany, from the Tigris and from North Africa. One Roman emperor was a Negro. So that a considerable amount of new blood entered the British racial stock during the Roman occupation, as at all other times in their long history.

We hope we have given enough examples to show that the Roman occupation of Gaul and Britain was not a trivial happening, but the broad base on which, after the Dark Ages, Western Europe was able to rebuild her foundations. The development of Gothic and Renaissance styles was derived from the memories of Rome, but this does not explain why, when the Romans came here in A.D. 43, they had so much to offer us. It is here that the romance of the period comes in. The great central fact about the Roman civilization is that by their earlier conquests they had inherited the wisdom of the ancient Near East, Egypt and Babylonia, the Israelites and Assyrians, the Minoans, Mycenaeans, and Achaeans; the Medes and Persians had all in their time contributed to a civilization which made its supreme bid for power, and met its defeat at the hands of the Greeks at Salamis in 480 B.C. When the Romans conquered the Greeks, a great fund of knowledge, which was becoming scientific and systematic, was placed at their disposal.

We begin with the popular modern subject of town-planning. Hippodamus of Miletus laid out Piraeus, the port of Athens, in the fifth century B.C. in a rectangular plane, and Alexander the Great was a town-planner. Dinocrates, his architect, laid out Alexandria (page 24).

The Romans were not only very good planners, as we can see by Fig. 6 of Silchester, but they paid great attention to public health and sanitation. They constructed sewers; the Cloaca Maxima in Rome can still be traced from the Forum of Nerva to its outflow into the Tiber. So far as medicine is concerned, Hippocrates, the great Greek doctor, was born as early as 460 B.C., and seems to have practised this profession as a doctor does today, with an outlook which was scientific and free from quackery. The earliest scientific medical work of the Romans seems to have been *De re Medica* of Celsus, about 30 B.C. This deals with the history of medicine, diet, disease, dentistry, and difficult and dangerous operations. The Roman bath at Bath was not only a bathing establishment but the earliest known English medical cure.

If we turn to architecture the Roman debt to the Greeks is equally apparent. The Greeks evolved their three Orders of Architecture (Figs. 3–5); if we turn to Figs. 18–21, we shall find that the Romans adopted their 'orders', altering them somewhat in detail, and adding one more (Fig. 20), the Composite, which was a fusion of Ionic and Corinthian, and these orders are still used.

Our Christian churches can be traced back to the Roman basilica, as described on page 35. There is hardly anything which we do today which cannot be traced back to Greece through Rome.

A very interesting day could be spent in a visit to

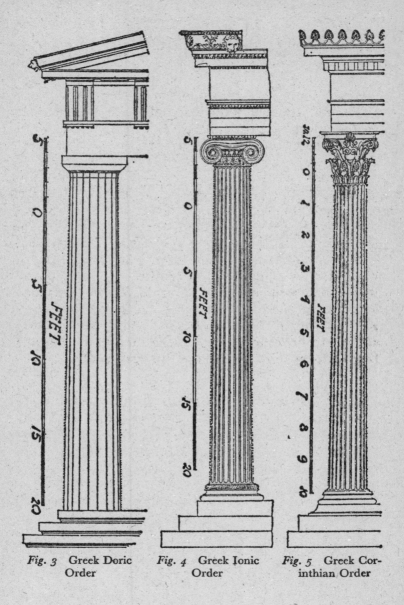

Fig. 3 Greek Doric Order

Fig. 4 Greek Ionic Order

Fig. 5 Greek Corinthian Order

the Glastonbury Museum, where are all the primitive things which were discovered in the Lake Village. An hour's run in the car would take us to the great Roman bathing establishment of the Romans at Bath (Fig. 12) – an amazing contrast to Glastonbury. In the afternoon, there would be time to go to Bradford-on-Avon and see the little Saxon church there. Centuries had to pass before the Saxons were able to build even such a simple structure as this. There could be no better illustration of the meaning of the Dark Ages which followed the fall of Rome – from the glory that was Greece to the grandeur that was Rome, and then back to this simple little church. Still, out of it Gothic architecture did develop. And then, while in Bradford, we could see The Hall there – an Elizabethan home which shows a renaissance of classical detail even more. A bird's-eye view, or pageant if you will, of the development of English architecture, and all to be seen in one day, in one small corner of England, by those who have the eyes to see.

2

SILCHESTER AND THE OTHER ROMAN TOWNS

CALLEVA ATREBATUM, Calleva (the town in the wood) of the Atrebates (Fig. 6) was planned on regular symmetrical lines. Silchester, as we call it now, was town-planned, and here for the first time we meet the chequer-board type of planning in this country. It presents a marked difference to the plan of Glastonbury Lake Village, which we saw in *Prehistoric Times*; there it was haphazard arrangement, with less sense of order.

If we try to trace the evolution of the chess-board type of plan, we are led back from Rome to Greece, and the work of Alexander the Great. He was a great town-planner, and his influence can be traced in the design of the cities of Asia Minor. The straight streets commended themselves to the soldier, because this was the manner in which he was accustomed to lay out his camps. In Roman times the soldier was much more than a mere fighter; he was, in fact, the handyman of the day, and could plan a town, build walls, and carry out engineering works. When Roman soldiers retired it was a practice to gather them together, and grant them land, as a reward for their services; then they built a town, and became a bulwark to the State; Timgad in the province of Numidia, in Roman Africa, was such a city. In more

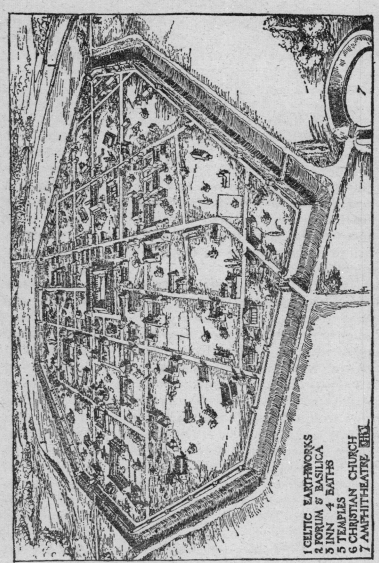

1 CELTIC EARTHWORKS
2 FORUM & BASILICA
3 INN   4 BATHS
5 TEMPLES
6 CHRISTIAN CHURCH
7 AMPHITHEATRE

Fig. 6 Silchester (Calleva Atrebatum)

ways than one the power of Rome depended on its legionaries, and we like to think of them, when their fighting days were over, building and carpentering, and showing the natives that their strong arms were attached to cunning hands.

It is quite evident that the Romans, wherever they went for their inspirations, were accomplished surveyors. No matter how well a road is made and finished, it has to be begun by someone, who determines its direction, and settles the gradients; a town cannot be laid out until men come along and peg out the lines of its streets and walls. This brings up the question of mensuration. The surveyor must instruct the constructor; he must say, for example, 'Here is the main street of your town, it is so many somethings wide.'

In these days of plenty, we are accustomed to travel about with bulging pockets, full of rules, rods, and tape measures, but this was not the case in the days long before Rome. Men used something which they could always be sure of having with them, to wit, their feet, and by Roman times, this habit had passed from custom into law. Vitruvius, writing in the time of Augustus said: 'It is worthy of remark, that the measures necessarily used in all buildings and other works, are derived from the members of the human body, as the digit, the palm, the foot, the cubit.' The normal Roman foot was 296 mm., or a full 11⅝ English inches. There were 16 digits, and 4 palms in the Roman foot, and the cubit was 6 palms, or 1½ feet. Five Roman feet went to the *passus* (pace), and 1000 of the latter to the mile.

In the same way the numerals have been derived from the hand with its five fingers. The Roman V is thought to have been simplified from a drawing of the

hand meaning 5. IV would mean the hand less one
finger, or 4; and VI the hand plus one or 6, and X a
double hand or 10.

When it came to measuring land, the Roman
thought of the feet of his oxen rather than his own, so
the unit he used was the iugerum, or yokeland; the
oxen ploughed a furrow 120 Roman feet long, before
they wanted a rest, and 120 by 120 formed the actus.
Two square actus, or 120 by 240, was the day's
ploughing, and this became the iugerum, which was
the unit of the Roman land surveyor. The Roman
dealt in land in blocks, which he could size up in his
mind, and readily estimate the crops which could be
grown. Mensuration, as most other subjects, is full of
interest, if you go to work to discover it. Here in
England, our furlong is a furrow long, equal to one
eighth of a mile, or 40 rods, poles, or perches; this rod
of 16½ feet has played a great part in English mensuration, and we shall have something to say of it later on.

Below we have set out in tabular form the Roman
measures:

Feet.	Gradus.	Passus.	Decempeda.	Actus.	Iugerum.	Stadium.	Mile.
2½ =	1						
5 =	2 =	1					
10 =	4 =	2 =	1				
120 =	48 =	24 =	12	= 1			
240 =	96 =	48 =	24	= 2	= 1		
625 =	250 =	125				= 1	
5000 =	2000 =	1000 =	500				= 1

and the Roman mile was 1617 English yards.

In founding a Roman city, the plough was used to
trace the outline of its walls, and it was inaugurated
by the augur, who consecrated the templum, or

centre square; here the cardo, running from north to south, was crossed by the decumanus from east to west. The four quarters of the town, around these main streets, were divided up into rectangular blocks, of which the iugerum was the general unit.

The surveyor, who was responsible for the layout of the city, used an instrument called the groma (Fig. 7). This consisted of a staff, with a cross turning on its top, from the ends of which small plummets were suspended by cords. These plummets came at the corners of a square, and it was the cords by which they were suspended that were used to sight the lines the surveyor wished to set out. His method was to send his assistants to hold rods which were stuck in the ground, where they were sighted as being on the line. It is obvious that the square line that the Romans liked so much could be set out very readily. Once the lines were set out, a 10-foot rod was used, and 12 of these gave the actus of 120 feet. Surveyors today use an instrument founded on the groma, which they call a cross-head staff.

Silchester (Fig. 6) was not a Roman municipality. There seem to have been only six of these in Britain, four of which were colonial (colonies of veteran soldiers) – Camulodunum (Colchester), Lindum (Lincoln), Glevum (Gloucester), Eburacum (York) – and two municipia (specially recognized settlements already in existence) – Verulamium

Fig. 7 Roman surveyors (Agrimensores or Gromatici) using the groma

(St. Albans) and, probably, Rotis (Leicester). The remainder of the country, except for imperial estates such as the lead mines of the Mendips, was organized in civitates which followed approximately the old tribal divisions, with the chiefs as magistrates. Local self-government was encouraged everywhere, and the main difference between these civitates and the municipalities was that the members of the latter were Roman citizens. The distinction, however, ceased to have real meaning when in 212 the Emperor Caracalla gave Roman citizenship to all freeborn provincials. Silchester must have been the civitas of the Atrebates. The town was rebuilt in its Roman form, with chessboard regularity, at about the end of the first and beginning of the second centuries, and, situated as it is (Fig. 1), on the top of a rounded hill, in pleasant country, and at the intersection of busy roads must have been a place of importance.

Let us imagine that we are paying a visit to Calleva Atrebatum. We approach the town by the road from the north, and on the outskirts we pass a funeral party going to bury its dead, outside the walls at the side of the road as was the Roman custom. Close up to the town, at 1, Fig. 6, is a ditch and bank, which may be the remains of the old British earthworks that had surrounded the tribal stronghold long before the days of the Romans. Like many British earthworks, these banks and ditches follow the contour lines of the hill, and are not square. The British earthworks influenced the layout of the stone walls, which were added at some later date than the rebuilding in Roman times; thus the streets are Roman in their chequer pattern, and the walls are British in their plan.

As we pass along outside the walls, we notice that they are about 20 feet high, built of concrete rubble,

and faced with flints; they are strengthened with
bonding courses of ironstone, and finished at the
bottom with chamfered stone bases. There are
rampart walks on the tops of the walls, with embrasures
through which the watchmen can see the approach
of strangers; at the base of the wall is a ditch 12 feet
deep and 80 feet wide.

When we are inside the walls, we shall find that
these are 9 feet 6 inches broad at base, lessened by set-
offs inside to about 7 feet 6 inches at the top, and at
about 200 feet intervals the full thickness of the wall
is carried up, like a wide buttress, and on these are
placed watch towers. To further strengthen the walls,
a mound of earth has been placed against them inside.

By this time we have arrived at the West Gate
(Fig. 8). The town, or curtain, walls are curved in-
wards on to two towers, and so take the form of
bastions, from which the bridge over the ditch can be
raked. Between the towers are double archways of 12
feet span, at 1 on the plan; at 2 is a guard-room, with
a lock-up behind it at 3. The other side of the plan is
at the rampart level, and shows how the guard can
pass from the top of the walls at 4, through the towers
at 5, and over the archways at 6.

If we now pass through the gate, it may be as well
to consult Fig. 6, and imagine that it is the plan of
Calleva Atrebatum, scratched in a tablet which has
been lent to us by the keeper of the gate. We will
follow the road which goes due east, until it crosses
another running from the North to the South Gate,
and here we will turn to the right. Almost immediately,
at 2 on the plan, we shall come to a building, which by
its size shows itself to be a place of importance, and on
inquiry we find that it is the basilica; however, we will

Fig. 8 The West Gate of Silchester

defer our inspection of the city until we have found an inn at which we can stay, and by consulting our map we see that there is one a little way ahead at 3.

The inn turns out to be a place rather like the house we describe on page 57, except that it has more accommodation, and has baths attached. We hear that there are larger baths, at 4 on the plan; so after leaving our bags at the inn, we go on to these, so that we may refresh ourselves after our journey.

Fig. 9 shows the plan of the building we find there. We enter a courtyard with a colonnaded walk around it, and this leads into the apodyteria, or dressing-rooms; here we take off our clothes and give our valuables into the care of an attendant. We then go into the frigidarium, or cold room; here we see men who have finished their baths, plunging into the cold bath, so that they may not catch cold on going into the open air; our readers know, of course, that the Roman bath consists of going into a series of rooms, heated with hot air, and this heat induces very generous perspiration.

We next enter the tepidarium which is fairly warm, and then the caldarium, which is really quite hot; here there is a bath of hot water, and at one end a basin of cold water, with which to splash oneself before passing out. It is here that we are anointed with oils, and our bodies massaged and scraped with strigils; then we, in our turn, pass back to the frigidarium and have our cold plunge, and sit about to watch the goings-on. Seneca, the philosopher, writing about A.D. 57, gives a better idea of life as seen in a Roman bath than we can. He said:

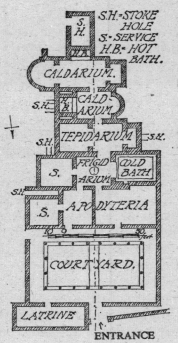

Fig. 9 Plan of the Baths at Silchester

I am living near a bath: sounds are heard on all sides. Just imagine for yourself every conceivable kind of noise that can offend the ear. The men of more sturdy muscle go through their exercises, and swing their hands heavily weighted with lead: I hear their groans when they strain themselves, or the whistling of

laboured breath when they breathe out
after having held in. If one is rather lazy,
and merely has himself rubbed with un-
guents, I hear the blows of the hand
slapping his shoulders, the sound varying
according as the massagist strikes with
flat or hollow palm. If a ball-player begins
to play and to count his throws it's all up
for the time being (then follows an amusing
note), or there is some one in the bath
who loves to hear the sound of his own
voice . . . but the hair-plucker from time
to time raises his thin shrill voice in order to attract
attention, and is only still himself when he is forcing
cries of pain from some one else, from whose armpits
he plucks the hairs.

Fig. 10
Strigil

Fig. 11 shows the exterior of the baths at Silchester,
and for a small town they are fine buildings, unless,
of course, they are compared with those at Bath, or
Aquae Sulis. Here the hot springs of healing waters
have been conducted to great basins in which the
people can bathe, and grouped around these are the
ordinary rooms of a Roman bath as at Silchester. We
give a sketch (Fig. 12) of the Great Bath, taken from
the east end. So far as we can judge this bathing-pool
must have been open to the sky when it was first
built, with a colonnaded walk around, as at A on the
sketch. Later it was roofed in with a vault made of
concrete reinforced with hollow tiles, and to carry
this, large stone piers were added at B. By cross
vaults the architect contrived that these piers at B
took all the weight of the vault, adding arches at the
back to take up any outward thrust; these were carried
on piers, one of which is shown at C.

T–B

Fig. 11 Baths at Silchester

The parts remaining of this vault at Bath give the best example we have in England of the Roman use of concrete reinforced with brickwork. In Rome itself the baths of Diocletian and Caracalla, the basilica of Constantine, and the Pantheon, are examples of vaults which are wonderful in their immense scale and permanence. It is very doubtful if any of the modern concrete work, reinforced with steel, will last even one hundred years against the insidious rust.

After our bath, being in good order, we go to the church, there to return thanks for our safe journey, and we find that the citizens of Calleva, very soon after the Edict of Toleration of the Emperor Constantine in 313, set about building themselves a Christian church. This is shown at 6 on Fig. 6.

The plan of the church (Fig. 13) is of what is known as the 'basilican type', which means that it resembles the basilica (Fig. 24). The points of resemblance are that the main body is divided into a

Fig. 12 The Great Bath at Bath

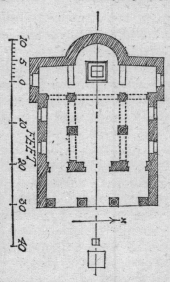

Fig. 13 Plan of the Christian church at Silchester

nave, with an aisle on each side, and the tribune of the basilica has become the apse of the church. The plan shows the beginning of transepts, which give the church its cruciform, or cross-like character.

It is worth considering how this came about. Take a sheet of paper and try to design anything you like; you may start with the idea that you are going to be wildly original, and then you will discover that originality consists of minute variations and improvements on what has gone before, and you will be forced to go back to something you know as a base on which to build. This is precisely what the first builders of Christian churches did; they started by adopting the basilica, because it was the building in which they had been used to assemble; the interest to us is that the little church at Silchester is the forerunner of our glorious Gothic cathedrals.

We must remember that the Society of Antiquaries, who excavated Silchester, only discovered the foundations of the building; the reconstruction built on these is our own. We will enter the church, and our first impression (Fig. 15) is one of surprise at the tiny size of the building; the nave, including the apse, is only 29 feet long by 10 feet wide; the aisles are 5 feet wide. The nave has a mosaic floor, the tesserae of which are red tiles 1 inch square; where the altar stands is a very beautiful panel of chequers in black, red, and white, and this part of the floor is not raised above the nave.

Let us now leave our imaginary walk and look at the drawings. Fig. 14 is a reconstruction, built up on the plan about which there is no doubt. For the super-structure, we have gone to Rome. After Constantine's Edict of Toleration, church building went forward, and the Christians had no need to lurk in byways. It is to this period that we can assign the five patriarchal basilicas, of St. Peter, St. John Lateran, Ste. Maria

Fig. 14 Exterior of the church at Silchester

Maggiore, St. Paul, and St. Lorenzo, beyond the walls at Rome. The old basilica of St. Peter was pulled down at the end of the fifteenth century to make room for the present church, and the others have been altered many times, yet sufficient remains to show what the early churches were like. Constantine is supposed to have helped dig the founda-tions of St. John Lateran with his own hands.

Fig. 15   Interior of the church at Silchester

The Silchester church was a much simpler building; its flint walls, with tile angles outside, were plastered inside, and painted in imitation of marble.

During Mass the priest stood facing eastwards behind the altar, which was probably a wooden table.

In the larger basilican churches it was usual for the clergy to be seated around the apse behind the altar, but there is hardly room for this arrangement at Silchester, and they probably used the nave together with the choir. Men and women were seated separately in the aisles. It will be noticed that there is a very large porch, or narthex. Here, with the doors open, were gathered the people not yet admitted to full communion.

This narthex, in the larger basilican churches, like St. Peter's, formed one side of a square courtyard, or atrium, which stood in front of the church. There is a splendid example at the later church of St. Ambrogio in Milan, and another delightful one at St. Clemente in Rome.

We cannot be sure if there was such a court at Silchester, but a foundation was discovered in front of the porch, with a little pit behind it, and this is thought to have been the base on which stood a laver, or labrum, where the worshippers could wash their hands, the pit having a drain connected with it. This laver may have been placed centrally in an eastern court, paved with flint pitching, of which part remains. Silchester church was built between 313 and the withdrawal of the Romans about a century later, and a similar building has been found at Caerwent (Venta Silurum) in Monmouthshire.

Here and there in England, smaller Christian relics of Roman date have been discovered. One of the most interesting of these is the pewter bowl in the British

Fig. 16 Sacred
Monogram,
Chi-Rho

Museum, discovered in the well of a Roman house at Appleshaw, near Andover, not far from Silchester. This bowl has the sacred monogram, Chi-Rho, composed of the two first Greek letters of the name Christ (Fig. 16) engraved on its base.

Apart from the town churches or basilicas, built specifically for Christian worship, we know something of how the needs of Christians were served in rural districts from the excavations at the Roman villa at Lullingstone in Kent. Here two or more rooms appear to have been set aside for Christian use during the fourth century. Fragments of painted wall plaster also decorated with the sacred Chi-Rho monogram have been found, and also figures of saints or pilgrims with their arms extended on either side in the early Christian attitude of prayer.

There are hints, in writings of the period, of British converts to Christianity early in the third century. St. Alban was martyred in 304, and three British bishops attended the Council of Arles in 314, which is evidence that, by this time, the converts had organized a Church. Then we have St. Patrick, the 1462nd anniversary of whose death was recognized on March 17th, 1924 by the dedication of a mosaic to his memory in the Houses of Parliament at Westminster. St. Patrick's name was Sucat, and he was the son of Calpurnius, a Roman official, who was a deacon of the Church, and whose father had been a priest. St. Patrick was born about 373, either in Dumbarton, or Glamorganshire, and was carried off by slave raiders to Ireland when a youth. Here he stayed six years, and then escaped to Gaul, whence, being trained in the Church, he went to Rome, and finally returned on his mission to the Irish about 437 or 438, where the Christians stood in need of his help.

We shall write later of the influence of the Irish Church, but sufficient has been said now to show that the Christian Church in this country was not the work of Augustine only.

There were four temples at Silchester in pre-Christian days, and these are shown at 5, Fig. 6. Fig. 17 illustrates one of these near the East Gate. During the excavations of the Society of Antiquaries, the foundations of a platform, 73 feet square, were discovered. The platform itself was $7\frac{1}{2}$ feet high, and in the middle of it stood the cella, which was 42 feet square outside, and 36 feet inside. The drawing is our reconstruction based on this plan.

The foundations of what must have been a very beautiful and interesting temple were discovered to the south of the basilica. The platform here had a regular 16-sided plan of 65 feet diameter. The cella placed centrally on this was 35 feet 7 inches in diameter, with walls which were 2 feet 6 inches thick, and 16-sided externally. This left space for the cella to be surrounded by a colonnaded walk or peristyle, 9 feet 6 inches wide, and the effect must have been like the temple of Vesta at Tivoli, or the beautiful one in the Forum Boarium at Rome.

Now that we are writing of temples, it may be well to make reference to the Orders of Architecture which the Romans used in their construction. We illustrated those of the Greeks on page 22. The Romans adopted them, but changed them as they went along. The Doric (Fig. 18) from the theatre of Marcellus at Rome, has been used in Figs. 14 and 17. The Ionic, also from the theatre of Marcellus, was as Fig. 19.

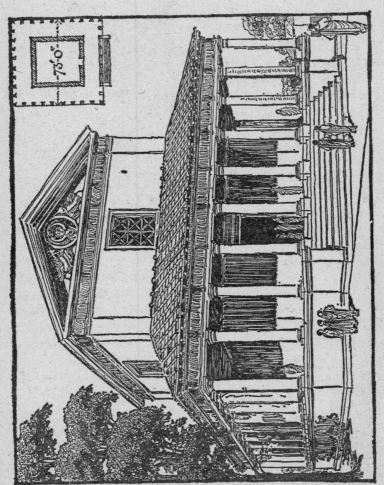

Fig. 17 One of the temples at Silchester

The Corinthian, from the Pantheon, Rome, was as Fig. 21; and the Composite, from the Arch of Titus, Rome (Fig. 20) was, as its name shows, composed of a fusion of Ionic and Corinthian. These Orders, together with the arch, were the raw materials with which the Roman architect worked, and his finished products, in the way of buildings, are the main inspiration of his successor of today.

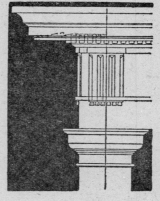

Fig. 18   Roman Doric Order
(theatre of Marcellus, Rome)

If it had been possible for us to walk the streets of Roman Silchester, as we at first pretended, after breakfasting at our inn we should go to the basilica to transact the business which brought us to the town. The basilica, as we have seen (Fig. 6, 2), stood in the centre of the east side of the street running through the town from north to south; if we go two islands to the west, and two to the east, and then take two north and south, we find that the streets are planned on a regular square. If Silchester had been a purely Roman town, this square would have been walled in, as was Caerwent in Monmouthshire, close to Caerleon, where the Second Legion was stationed. It rather looks as if this central portion at Silchester

Fig. 19   Roman Ionic Order
(theatre of Marcellus, Rome)

Fig. 20 Roman Composite
Order (Arch of Titus, Rome)

Fig. 21 Roman
Corinthian Order
(Portico of
Pantheon, Rome)

was the first portion built, as early
as A.D. 70–85, and the walls, enclosing
about 100 acres, were built at a later
date to follow the lines of the British
earthworks.

The broadest roads in the town
were about 28½ feet wide, and formed
of a bed of hard gravel, pitched with
flints in the centre, to form a gutter.

The basilica formed part of a group
of buildings (Fig. 22). This plan is
very remarkable and shows us that the
Romans were quite used to buildings
planned on an axial line, with a
sense of dignity and order. We know that there had
not been any such building done in England before

the time of the Romans, and after them we have to wait till the sixteenth century before we find these ideas again.

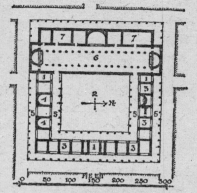

Fig. 22 Plan of the forum and basilica at Silchester

The gateway (Fig. 22, 1), led into the forum, or Greek agora (Fig. 23). This was the market place of the town, and around it were shops (Fig. 22, 3). Here the slaves came to do their marketing, and the country people set up little booths. It was used as well for games, and gladiatorial contests before the amphitheatre was built. The municipal offices were at 4, and colonnaded walks at 5. These connected with the basilica at 6. This consisted of a fine hall, about 233 feet long by 58 feet wide; here the merchants met to do business. At each end were the semicircular tribunes where justice was administered. In the centre of the west side was the curia, or the council chamber of the city, with other halls and offices, at 7.

Fig. 24 shows what the interior of the basilica looked like. This reconstruction is possible because part of one of the Corinthian capitals was found, and this settled the diameter of the columns. In Roman architecture the height of a column bears a definite relation to its diameter, and again the entablature over, consisting of architrave, frieze, and cornice, has a definite proportion. During the excavations, portions of Purbeck marble and an imported white marble were found, and it is thought that these were used for

Fig. 23 The forum and basilica at Silchester

wall linings. The portions not treated in this way were plastered, and painted gaily with light red, yellow, white, blue, and green. The world has only become grey in colour since the Industrial Revolution.

We will here insert a reminder that before the Christian era, a basilica was a place such as we have described, but that after, the word was used at times for a church.

This group of buildings, in more ways than one, formed the civic centre. It is interesting to remember that the word civilization comes from *civis*, a citizen, one who had mastered the art of living in a town. The Atrebates seem to have managed it very well; better, in fact, than we do today, with our hopeless struggle to make the dreadful industrial towns fit places in which to live.

During the excavations no trace of buildings was found to the south of the basilica, behind the church. This space may have been the cattle market, and another open space on the east may have been used for the farmers' carts.

Silchester does not provide us with a specimen of one of the great accomplishments of the Romans, the arched bridge. It is a great pity that they did not feel

Fig. 24 The interior of the basilica, Silchester

tempted to span the Thames with bridges like the Pons Ælius and Pons Fabricius at Rome.

Before we study the smaller details of Silchester, it would be as well if we again looked at its layout (Fig. 6), and consider what it means. True, there are the later walls, added when times were becoming troublous, but even with these it presents a very civilized picture. It is not dominated by a castle, with moat and drawbridges, as was the case with the towns which were built in the Middle Ages. The people of Silchester may have needed protection from raiders, but nobody frowned at them from inside. Here they were able to lead a life which was free, and gave them opportunities to develop their own individual tastes. Later the Barbarian raids forced men together in packs, and a common fear made them wolfish; the monastery was to become the one place in which a man could do quiet work, and the cloak of religion the only substitute for a sharp sword. The world had to wait a thousand years or more before it was to see again any town planned on such kindly lines as Silchester.

Viroconium, like Silchester, was a great Roman town in which the British element is evident in the nature of its plan, and in other ways; but both its beginning and its end are wrapped in mystery. It is thought to have been the base from which the attack on the Ordovices of North Wales was launched, a base which was later moved to Chester (Deva), where the great fortress was built, which was occupied for so long by the Twentieth Legion. As to its end, the general opinion is that it was sudden, overwhelming, and tragic, an onslaught by fire and sword. One of the most startling clues to this idea was found in the heating chamber of the baths, where, among the small forest of pillars which carried the floor of the heated room above the floor of the furnace chamber some skeletons were found huddled together. They had evidently been suffocated by the fumes. That they had come here as a last resort to escape from a worse death, was seen by the fact that they had brought their small store of earthly treasure with them – the skeleton of an old man still clutched a bag of coins. The disaster is placed in the fifth century, but whether the enemy was the Pict, the Scot, or the Saxon is unknown.

As at Silchester, no town was ever again built on the site of Viroconium. The village of Wroxeter stands to one side of the ruined city, and is but a tiny place. But much of the church is built with material from the Roman buildings, and the font is hollowed out of an upturned base from one of the columns of the forum. Silchester, as we have seen (page 24), was a town of the British tribe Atrebates; Viroconium was a town of the Cornovii, as is clearly set forth in the finest lettered inscription ever found in Britain, whose place was over the entrance to the forum. Out of the great quantity of things found here, one of the most interesting is a soldier's discharge-book. It is not quite a book in our sense of the word, being graven on a small sheet of copper. But it evidently answered the same purpose as the discharge-book which is handed to the present-day soldier when his time of service in the army is expired. It runs as follows:

The Emperor, Caesar Trajanus Hadrianus Augustus, son of the deified Trajanus, grandson of the deified Nerva, Chief Pontiff, holding the Tribuncian Power for the nineteenth time. Consul for the third time, Father of his Country.

To THE Cavalry and Infantry who have served

in six cavalry regiments and thirty-one infantry regiments which are called – (names given but many indecipherable) and are in Britain under Publius Mummius Sisenna; who have served for twenty-five or more years, and have been discharged with an honourable discharge, whose names are written below:—HAS GIVEN citizenship for themselves, their children, and their descendants, and the right of legal marriage with the wives they then possessed when citizenship was given to them, or if any of them are bachelors with those whom they may hereafter marry up to the number of one apiece.

April 14th

In the Consulship of L. Tutilius Pontianus and C. Calpurnius Atilianus (A.D. 135).

Of the Second Cohort of Dalmatians commanded by ... Julius Maximus of Rome.

To the ex-footsoldier

Mansuetus, son of Lucius of the neighbourhood of Trier.

Copied and checked from the bronze tablet which is fixed in Rome on the wall behind the temple of the deified Augustus near Minerva's temple.

So runs this magnificent rigmarole which is a certified true copy of a bronze tablet put up in Rome – such was the efficiency of the Records Department of the War Office of ancient Rome. Every soldier honourably discharged had such a tablet erected and could have a certified true copy to keep by him if he chose to pay for it. When the present document in copper was prepared, one can sense from the couching of the official language how the ex foot-soldier, Mansuetus, son of Lucius, was much the least important person mentioned. Yet, after all these years, it is his name alone which fires our imagination, because he has presented himself to us as a personality (if a very ordinary one) with a name, who lived in that long-forgotten city of Britain. Here is a man *with a name* who lived in old Wroxeter eighteen hundred years ago! We know a little more from the date and the various regiments quoted (and some of these proud fighting units we should never have heard of but for Mansuetus). We know, for instance, that he served as a member of the garrison in that fort on Hadrian's Wall which in his time was called Magnae and is now called Carvoran. Magnae is ruined, Viroconium buried, the Empire vanished. But this scrap certifying the honourable discharge of Mansuetus, son of Lucius, is still with us, as good as new, and it may outlast the skyscrapers of New York, concrete though they be.

In Viroconium one may perhaps trace something of the answer to that interesting riddle of *how a town comes to be*. If our guess is right that the attack on North Wales was launched from here, and that the Romans had at first intended the fort they founded here to be the home of a legion (though the plan was changed and Chester made the legionary fortress), then we have the nucleus. After the foundation of Chester, Viroconium would have a double reason for prosperity. For the natural resources of the countryside of Shropshire are rich, and the garrison at Chester, although some forty miles away, would afford it a measure of protection. Now, although the town was wiped out (as we guess) and its site became a desert, the tradition and the developed system of its trade was evidently not lost. These were merely transferred to an adjacent site better protected by natural barriers. The new location chosen was at the bend of the Severn, where the river forms an isthmus, then known as Pengwern and now called Shrewsbury; and its motto, *Floreat Salopia*, still holds good.

Another interesting example of a civil town with something akin in its history is to be seen in South Wales. This is Venta Silurum, now called Caerwent. It also has a neighbour in a great legionary fortress, namely, that at Caerleon (Isca Silurum), but the distance in this case is only a matter of seven miles. Though the buildings at Caerwent have mostly been excavated there is less to see there than at Viroconium, except for one grand feature which is lost to view in the Shropshire town. That is the walls. The south and west walls at Caerwent are one of the best examples of their kind in Britain. In some respects they are unique and they are now preserved as an ancient monument by the Ministry of Works. What the fate of this town was after the end of the Roman occupation of Britain is not known. Probably it was not so sudden and disastrous as that of Viroconium. But in spite of its walls it came to an end as a trade centre, though there seems to be good evidence that here again there was a transfer and the business faculty moved from Caerwent to Chepstow.

Caerleon (Caerwent's neighbour) was the home of the Second Legion. And, as was the custom at an important garrison town, there was an amphitheatre in which fights with wild beasts and between gladiators were 'put on'. Recent excavations have unearthed this building, which has been wonderfully preserved. The entrance, the dens of the beasts, are all to be seen. It is far the best example which we have. It is not the biggest, for that is at Chester, but excavation is here impossible because of the town.

At Colchester the Roman walls of the town are wonderfully well preserved. And here is to be seen the most perfect specimen which we have of a Roman gateway. At Colchester, too, is our only ruin of a large temple. It is very fragmentary, however, consisting only of the vaults of the foundation, for on top of it is built a Norman castle, the whole material of which is of Roman origin. There are many ruins of small temples that were raised to the gods of the British, but of the larger sort dedicated to the gods and the god-emperors of the official religion of Rome no remains exist except this single one at Colchester – it is thought to have been raised to the conqueror of Britain, the deified Emperor Claudius.

Colchester was the old chief metropolis of Britain before the Romans made London. Here reigned Cunobelinus, the Cymbeline of Shakespeare, father of Caractacus. And at Lexden, on the outskirts of Colchester, a tumulus has been excavated which contained the remains of so rich and grand a funeral that it could have been the grave of Cunobelinus himself.

3

THE PEOPLE AND THEIR HOUSES

THE time has come to write about the people who lived in these towns. We have set out our stage, and the drawings we have made must be accepted as the scenery. Against this background we will place our figures, but, alas, we cannot endow them with life, nor even jerk them with little strings, as marionettes, from the top of the stage. The imaginations of our readers must supply the motive power.

Magistrates, priests and freeborn children wore the toga prætexta, made of white wool, with a purple border. Under the toga came the tunica, with the purple border if the wearer was a senator. The toga developed from the cloak, which in early times had been the national garment, and in the Empire was the ceremonial dress of the upper classes. Linen was not used before the Empire.

Fig. 25 shows how the toga was put on. About 6 feet of the straight edge was placed over the left shoulder, the curved side being outside; the remaining part of the toga was passed round the body, under the right arm,

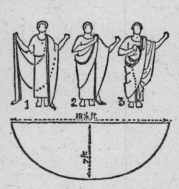

Fig. 25   Pattern and method of putting-on of the toga

and then thrown over the left shoulder
as 2. The part which hung down in
front from the left shoulder was then
pulled up under the fold across the
body as 3. Women wore the stola, a
form of tunica, with an undershift
(*subucula*), and their mantle was an
oblong-shaped piece of material. This
was the palla. The tunica was the in-
door garment for men and women;
sometimes, it was sleeveless, and then
the undershift had sleeves.

Fig. 26
Hair-dressing

Rough tunics were worn by shop-keepers and
workmen, and we must bear in mind that
mingling with the crowd we should have met
in Silchester would have been figures wearing
the old British costume we described in *Prehistoric Times*. British men often wore in addition
the hooded cloak (*paenula*), a very useful out-
door garment. This hood was to remain until in
the fourteenth century it was lengthened into
the liripipe, hanging from the chaperon, and
finished by snuggling down into a turban.

As well as sandals, heavy leather shoes stud-
ded with nails were worn. Fig. 26 shows a
method of hair-dressing which was fashionable
in the days of the early Empire, and Fig. 27
is a carved bone pin which may have been used
for the hair.

In *Prehistoric Times* we traced the very beautiful developments of the brooch (*fibula*): how,
from a simple safety-pin, it became a very
elaborate affair with bilateral springs. These
continued in Roman times, but in the early
Empire we find hinged brooches (Fig. 28). The

Fig. 27
Bone
pin

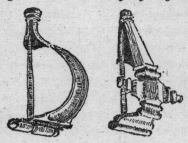

Fig. 28   Bronze brooches

ones illustrated were made of bronze, and then tinned to look like silver.

Had we been walking round Silchester in Roman times, we should not have found all the people in togas to be pure Romans, and those in tunics, Britons. If we remember how small a State was the original Rome, we can see that there would not have been enough Romans to go round. One of the ways in which the genius of the Romans was shown was their ability to absorb very varying peoples into their midst, and endow them with the Roman spirit. The great Trajan himself was a Spaniard. Fig. 66 shows the tombstone of a legionary, who, though he was born in Macedonia, lived and died in Lincoln. He may have had a British wife, and told his Romano-British children tales of what he did when he was a boy.

Having seen something of the people and their appearance, we can now pass to the Romano-British houses, and nowhere shall we find a better illustration of Roman skill. The Roman house of Italy was built round small courtyards to exclude the sun. The entrance from the street led into the first of these courtyards called the atrium, which was roofed over except for a central opening, the compluvium, above a shallow basin in the floor, the impluvium. There were small bedrooms at the sides of the atrium, and the tablinum, or reception-room, was opposite the entrance; this room also opened on to the peristyle at the back. This was the garden surrounded by colonnaded walks, at the far end of which, opposite the tablinum, was the exedra, which answered the same purpose as a modern drawing-room.

The Roman in Italy built his house around a courtyard, but in England he wisely realized that he could not afford to shut out the sun, and so opened up the whole plan. The so-called 'villa' was really a large self-contained country establishment, with its farm outbuildings. A number have been discovered and excavated in the southern part of England, and amongt hem we may mention as typical instances those at Lullingstone, Kent; Bignor, Sussex; Brading, Isle of Wight; North Leigh, Oxfordshire; and at Chedworth, Gloucester and Hambleden, near the Thames, where small museums have been built for the objects brought to light.

Fig 29 shows the plan of a Roman villa, at Spoonley Wood, well placed in a combe opening off the main escarpment of the Cotswolds, near Winchcombe, Gloucestershire.

Here we have the entrance at 1 leading into a large courtyard, or combination of atrium and peristyle, and this leads, as in the real Roman house, to the tablinum at 2. The triclinium, or dining-room, was at 3, with a specially heated

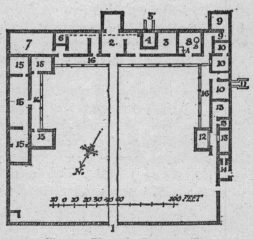

Fig. 29 Plan of a Roman villa

room, for use in winter, at 4. As the heat from the stoke-hole, 5, is taken under all the rooms to 6, these appear to have been reception-rooms. Room 7 was not heated, so may have been a summer-room. The kitchen was at 8, with larders and stores at 9. The three rooms at 10 are heated from the stoke-hole at 11, and so must have been for winter use, or for other branches of the family, living under the same roof. Rooms 12 and 13 were the bathrooms cut off from the house, with their own separate entrance from the courtyard. The three rooms, 13, were heated from a stoke-hole at 14, and were the frigidarium, tepidarium, and caldarium. At 12 was the cold bath, 16 feet by 11 feet 6 inches, quite big enough for a plunge and kick about. Evidently cleanliness ranked high as a virtue in Roman times; very much higher than in the time about which Thackeray wrote in *Pendennis*. Here the old Benchers in the Temple complained bitterly about the water which was spilled on the stairs when being carried up for Warrington's and Pendennis's baths; they had always managed to do without baths, why did these wretched youngsters want to go in for them? As Thackeray points out, our ancestors, of not so long ago, were the 'great unwashed'.

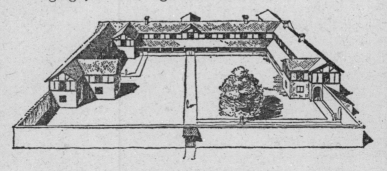

Fig. 30 Exterior of a Roman villa

The slaves' quarters are supposed to have been at 15, without any communication with the house, except through the courtyard. So far as the form of the plan is concerned, there is not any doubt at all;

Fig. 31   Girls playing knuckle-bones

when we come to the structure which was raised on it, we are on more debatable ground, and it may be well for us to describe how we have built up the exterior shown in Fig. 30. The colonnaded walks at 16 had dwarf columns standing on low walls. We know this because the columns which supported the roof were found at Spoonley Wood, 6½ inches diameter, and the Stonesfield slates with which it was covered. This is shown in more detail on Fig. 32. The same thing happened at Silchester. Here it was that a valuable clue was gained as to the construction of the upper floors. In excavating it was noticed that some of the ground floors were covered to the depth of a few inches with a layer of clay, which, on careful examination, showed marks of wattling. Wattle and daub construction is known to have been used at the Glastonbury Lake Village, and consisted of daubing a mixture of clay and chopped straw on to wattle hurdles, fitted in between timber framing. It was thought that the clay on the floors at Silchester was the remains of a timber-framed upper storey that had decayed and fallen down. The appearance of the upper part of a Roman house would have been rather like mediaeval half-timbering, though our drawing looks more like a golf pavilion of today.

Fig. 32   Courtyard of a Roman house

At Spoonley Wood, the ground-floor walls were
built of local stone, and average 2 feet thick, and in
almost all cases the walls of Roman houses were
covered with stucco and coloured. At one of the houses
recently excavated at Verulamium, it was possible to
recover nearly a whole stucco wall in fragments.
These have been mounted on a stand and are now in
the British Museum. The yellow stucco or plaster
wall is covered with a most beautiful running scroll
design decorated with beautifully painted peacocks.

This gives us some idea of the fashion in interior decoration in Roman times.

Fig. 33 shows the Roman triclinium, or dining-room, and how the diners reclined on low couches round a centre table. It seems an uncomfortable method of feeding.

We referred on page 58 to the heated floors at Spoonley Wood. Fig. 34 shows how this was done, and it was a very clever method. If an architect today is designing an operating theatre in a hospital, he adopts the Roman way of heating the floors and walls, because it prevents the humid air from condensing on the walls, which it will do if they are cold. The Roman architect started with a layer of concrete at A; on this he placed large tiles at B, and built thereon square piers, or *pilæ*, C. On these were placed as caps square tiles at D, and others were bridged across at E; on this the concrete floor was formed, with its mosaic covering.

The stoke-hole was outside, and here a slave made

Fig. 33 Roman triclinium or dining-room

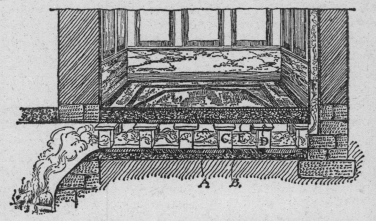

Fig. 34   Roman method of heating houses—by hypocaust

the fire, which he may have pushed right under the
floor, the degree of heat being settled by the amount
of floor which could be reached by the fire; if an
ordinary room, for use in winter, was to be heated,
then a duct from the furnace led to a central area,
from which other ducts led to the vertical wall flues; if
it was the caldarium, or hot room of a bath, then the
whole floor was suspended over the heating space, and
the wall flues were multiplied, and gathered into
chimneys much in the modern way.

Fig. 34 can be used to describe the way the Romans
decorated their rooms. The walls were plastered, and
then painted in very joyous colours. At Reading
Museum there are pieces of plaster found at Silchester,
showing traces of vivid colour, and painted decoration; these seem to be based on imitations of marbles,
and the effect, taken in conjunction with the mosaic
floors, must have been very fine.

The floors of the houses at Silchester were finished
in a variety of ways. In some mosaic was used. In

others, the final coat was formed with a cement made of lime and small fragments of broken brick, which was rubbed down to a smooth surface, and then polished; this was called *opus signinum*. The mosaic floors were formed of small cubes, of differently coloured materials: black and orange sandstones, white and grey limestones, yellow and red bricks, and Purbeck marble. Fig 35 shows the mosaic worker, cutting sawn sticks of these materials into the cubes, or tesserae; he holds the stick on the top of a chisel, set in a wooden block, and cuts the cubes by tapping with the hammer, just as the old-fashioned sweetstuff man used to do. The hammer and chisel were found at Silchester. The commoner floors were laid with larger cubes. If an old Roman floor is examined, it will be found to have a pleasant hand-made appearance, whereas modern mosaic looks like its imitation in oilcloth.

Windows were glazed at Silchester, and the glass appears to have been cast in moulds, in the shape of the panes; it is just one more illustration of the fascination of History; here we are writing of window glass, and scientifically heated houses and, in a century or so, the fabric of civilization itself crumbles away, and we must wait until the thirteenth century before we find glass again in this country, and our twentieth-century houses are not yet so well heated. For artificial light, candlesticks were used, and lamps in which oil was burned (Fig. 36).

Fig. 35   Mosaic worker

Fig. 36 A lamp

We can now think of the very important detail of cooking, and in Fig. 37 we see a gridiron, found at Silchester, and the method of using it. All cooking was done on a raised hearth made of masonry. One of these was found at Pompeii, with the pot in place, just as it was when destruction fell on the city. The charcoal used for fuel was kept in the arch below. The fire was made on this open hearth, and the charcoal fumes, which are dangerous, must have been carried away by a hood over the hearth into a wall flue. We are indebted to a friend for an account of how cooking was carried on in a Florentine kitchen, as late as 1893; the same open hearth as shown in our illustration was used. In this were small holes about 9 to 12 inches square, and 6 inches deep, in which fires were lighted, and pots boiled in the ordinary way, or food was fried, or grilled. Many vegetable dishes were used or just the leg of a chicken fried in olive oil. It was when any baking had to be done that trouble arose, because the Italian seldom bakes, but prefers frying and boiling; they do not go in for making puddings,

Fig. 37 Roman kitchen

but buy them at the cake shop. When they had to bake, or warm up anything, they used a *Forno di Campagna*, or oven of the country, which consisted of a large round pan, like a saucepan, standing on legs; this was put over the fire, and a flat cover being placed on the pan, another small charcoal fire was made on the top, and the cook, with a fan, regulated the amount of heat. This somewhat resembles the old west-country method and it may explain why it is that brick ovens are not found in the ruins of Roman houses in this country.

The Romans in this country may have been like the Florentines of 1893, and not such great meat-eaters as the barbarians they conquered.

The cook shown in Fig. 37 is making a sauce in a bronze skillet or saucepan, and a stew is simmering in the bronze cooking-pot. The large pots on the floor are used to keep oil and wine, and a flesh hook hangs from the end of the shelf. The oil-burning lamp was found at Newstead, a Roman fort near Melrose in Scotland. On the table is a lipped vessel called a

Fig. 38 Samian bowl

Fig. 39   Castor ware

mortar, which had pieces of grit worked into the surface of the clay before it was fired, so that vegetables and other food could be rubbed down in it. Corn continued to be ground into flour in mills as shown in *Prehistoric Times*.

Food was sent up to the table in what is perhaps the most typical of all Roman pottery, the fine red glazed ware we call Samian, or *Terra sigillata*. This was made originally at Arezzo in Tuscany, and then spread through the Empire, and being copied by the potters of Gaul, was imported into Britain. The ornament was impressed from a mould. Fig. 38 shows a typical shape. There are, in the British Museum, many specimens of plain Samian ware, which have been dredged up from the Pudding-Pan Rock near Whitstable, Kent, where they had been since the vessel which was bringing the pottery was wrecked in Roman times.

Castor ware (Fig. 39) was made at Castor, near Peterborough, so it is a peculiarly British pottery. It appears to have been founded on Samian, but it is copper or slate colour, and the white ornament in low relief is not cast as the Samian, but executed with a pipe like the sugar decoration on a wedding cake. This ornament has a freedom which is Celtic in its joyous curves. Fig. 40 shows a hunting scene from another Castor vase.

Fig. 40 Decoration on Castor ware

Very interesting pottery was made in the New Forest (Fig. 41); this was generally reddish-brown or black.

Fig. 42 shows some typical specimens of Roman glass. As was the case with the Samian ware of which we have been writing, the glass was first manufactured in the south of Gaul, and then, in the second century, in Belgium and at Cologne, and imported into Britain. This stimulated the British craftsmen, and it is thought that the simpler types which are found are their copies of the imported wares. A visit should be paid to the Roman-British Room at the British Museum, where can be seen a most wonderful pillar-moulded blue glass bowl. This was discovered quite recently on the Chiltern Hills, under a carriage drive. The bowl was only a few inches below the surface, and formed part of the furnishings of a grave. By a miracle the pick made a small round hole through the bowl, but did not crack it, so

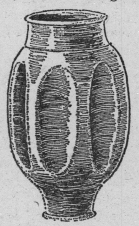

Fig. 41 New Forest pottery

Fig. 42   Roman glass

the Museum possesses the only complete bowl of that kind of glass found as yet in England.

Fig. 43 shows how the householder at Silchester provided himself with water. The drawing is a reconstruction of a force-pump found there. The rocking arm worked the pistons, which, moving up and down in their cylinders, sucked up the water from the well underneath, through the valves as shown. The descending piston shut one valve, and forced the water into the central reservoir through the other, and so up to the discharge pipe.

Great attention was paid to the details of sanitation. In Crete, Sir Arthur Evans discovered an excellent system which at a much earlier period made use of jointed drain-pipes; and underground sewers, flushed with water, were used by the Romans from a very early date.

From houses and home life, we can now turn to the trades and industries which supplied the inhabitants of Silchester with the everyday things they needed. The principal shops were in the forum, because this was the central meeting-place of the town, and they were very

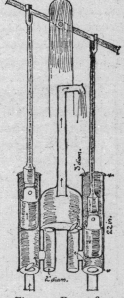

Fig. 43   Pump from Silchester

simply planned. The front was formed by a square opening in the wall (Fig. 44). In this was placed the counter, built of masonry, with a gap at one end through which the shopman could pass, the customer preferring to stand on the pavement. A staircase led directly out of the shop to an upper room, and sometimes there was another room at the back of the shop. The shops were closed by wooden shutters, placed in grooves at top and bottom, and overlapping much as they used to do in England until the advent of roller blinds in recent times.

Today if you go into the back streets of an Italian city, or one of the smaller towns, you can find the shops still remaining much as we have described. In the larger places, alas, the hideous output of modern industry is very barely veiled behind plate-glass, as in our own London.

Fig. 45 illustrates an interesting pair of scales found at Silchester. The beam is of bronze, about 13 inches long, and graduated on the top, so that the instrument

Fig. 44   A Roman shop

Fig. 45 Scales from Silchester

is a combination of steelyard and balance. Assuming that the fish being weighed is over 1 lb. in weight, a 1-lb. weight would be placed in the opposite pan, and another 1-lb. weight would be moved along the beam until the weight of the fish was balanced. If the fish were under 1 lb., then the 1-lb. weight would be placed in the opposite pan, and the other used on the beam, but this time on the same side as the fish. It was an extremely clever way of dispensing with many small weights.

The steelyard works on the laws of leverage we explained in *Prehistoric Times*. These may be summarized in the diagram on Fig. 46. Imagine that these are the beams of steelyards; a 1-lb. weight 12 inches from the point of suspension will be balanced by a 2-lb. one on the other side 6 inches away; again 1 lb. 12 inches away equals 4 lb. 3 inches away, and 1 lb. 12 inches away, equals 8 lb. only 1½ inches away. This will serve to explain the ingenuity of the Roman scale shown in Fig. 46.

Fig. 46 The Roman steelyard

The leg of lamb is hanging by hooks and chains to a ring with a movable collar on the beam. If something heavier had to be weighed, the man held the scale by the middle hook, turned the beam round and brought another graduated scale into use; by our diagram we see that with the same

Fig. 47 A butcher's shop

weight of 1 lb. at 12 inches, he could weigh 4 lb. at 3 inches, or 8 lb. at 1½ inches. This is the reason for the three handles. The butcher shown in Fig. 47 has a steelyard hanging up behind him, and while he cuts up the joints his wife enters the weights on a wax tablet with a stilus.

Interesting discoveries of tools were made at Silchester. In 1890, and again in 1900, when wells were being cleared out, hoards were discovered of very varying types. It is interesting to speculate how this came about. It is easy to understand how broken crockery, and other oddments, were found in wells and cesspools; a careless person would throw them down to get rid of them, but a careful workman would not do this with good tools. In 1854, at Great Chesterford, Essex, another hoard was found, 6 feet deep in a pit, so it looks as if in the perilous times either at the end of the Roman occupation, or during the Saxon Terror, the workman buried his tools, hoping to be able to come back some day and start work again, and as he was not able to do so, there they have lain until discovered by the archaeologist of today.

Fig. 48   Smiths and their tools

The actual tools found at Silchester can be seen at Reading Museum, and so we are enabled to show the Roman at work. Fig 48 shows a smith using a pair of tongs which are quite modern in type. Besides making his own tools, he would have made those for other tradesmen.

The carpenter shown in Fig. 49 has a metal-faced plane, 13½ inches long by 2½ inches broad, and was well provided with chisels, gouges, adzes, hammers, and axes; all the Silchester axes had hammer heads. He uses the same kind of saw as Italian carpenters of today. All the nails used would have been made by the smith. He made the mowers' anvils shown in Fig. 50; these were tapped into the ground, and used by men to temper the scythe with which they cut the corn. It is assumed that the strange-shaped implement the man is hammering, which was found at Great Chesterford, is a scythe; the one at the top of the picture from Newstead is a better shape.

The smith provided the iron last shown in Fig. 51, and with it the shoemaker mended shoes as shown.

The smith, in fact, must have been a very handy man; an adze was found (Fig. 49, 2) with a curved cutting edge, which suggests its use by coopers to hollow the staves of barrels. The coulter (Fig. 52, A) helped the ploughman, and points to an improvement on the plough described by Virgil in the *Georgics*; this consisted of a share beam to which was attached the iron share, B, the shaft with a yoke, and a vertical

Fig. 49 The carpenter and his tools

handle; not, in fact, very much different from the primitive type shown in *Prehistoric Times*. By the introduction of the coulter a vertical cut was made in the soil, and this could then be turned over far more easily by the ploughshare. We have attempted to show how we think the coulter was applied to the plough of the Romans (Fig. 52).

Fig. 50 Scythes and mower's anvil

The smith made large heavy padlocks of what seems to us an extraordinary pattern. Fig. 53 shows how these were operated. The key was inserted at the top into a slot, pushed into a vertical position, and was then forced down until it engaged with the four vertical rods shown by dotted lines. On the top of the rods were welded flat pieces of iron which were free to spring out at the bottom. The key was perforated to fit down over the ends of the rods, and being pushed down, compressed the flat springs, so that this portion could be drawn off A. We cannot say what the uses of the padlock were. At Great Chesterford five handcuffs were found, attached to a smaller padlock of the same pattern (Fig. 54); in the barracks of the gladiators at Pompeii, remains of stocks were found in the guardroom, which worked on much the same principle, so that here in England the padlocks were perhaps a means of discipline for slaves.

The Romans, being men of property, were quite used to locking up things. The simplest type of lock was one which had come down from Greek times, like

Fig. 51 **A shoemaker**

Fig. 52   A plough

the top sketch in Fig. 55. Here a long key was pushed through a vertical slot, then, being turned round, was hooked into two pegs or tumblers, 2, which being

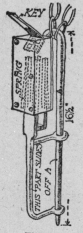

Fig. 53
A padlock

lifted up, allowed the bolt, 1, to be drawn back by a leather thong, 3, from the outside. In the centre sketch of Fig. 55, the pegs or tumblers, 2, are kept down into the bolt, 1, so that it is locked by a spring, 4; to unlock the bolt a key, rather like a tooth-brush at right angles to its handle, is placed under the bolt, so that the tumblers are pushed up, and the bolt can be drawn back by the key.

The sketch at the bottom of Fig. 55 shows how the tumbler type developed into the lever lock. The tumbler has become a projection on the underside of 2, which turns on a pin, and is kept in position by a spring at 3. The tumbler prevents

Fig. 54
Handcuffs

the bolt, 1, being shot back by dropping into a slot in it. The key is inserted and turned, and levers up the tumbler. The key is interesting as it can be worn on the finger as a ring.

Fig. 56 shows how the Roman boy saved up his money in an earthenware pot that had to be broken before he could get at the contents.

In the north-west part of the town at Silchester, there appear to have been dyers' workshops. Here were found remains of furnaces, built rather in the same way as old-fashioned brick-set coppers. Woad and madder were used by the dyers. The woad plant was cut up and washed, partly dried, and ground up into a paste, and allowed to ferment. The paste was formed into balls, dried in the sun, and then being collected into heaps, fermented and became hot and fell into a

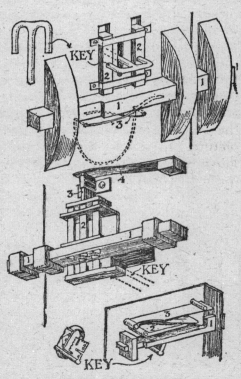

Fig. 55 Locks and keys

powder. The roots of the madder plant were dried and ground into powder.

Fig. 56
Money pot

The fullers were important people with the Romans. First they had to deal with the new cloth. This was washed with fuller's earth, to remove the oily matter in the wool of which most of the clothes were made; it was then stretched to make it even, again washed to shrink it, carded to make the nap and, any inequalities being cut off, was finally pressed.

One of the fulleries at Pompeii has pictures showing the different processes. The white woollen cloth was bleached by being stretched over a frame, and subjected to the fumes of sulphur burning in a pot below. In Fig. 8 a fuller is shown walking over the bridge into the town, carrying one of these bleaching-frames.

The fullers also dealt with the cleansing of dirty clothes. According to Mau, soap was a Gallic invention which had only begun to come into use at the time of the destruction of Pompeii, so in the pictures, to which we have referred, the fullers are shown at work doing the cleaning. The clothes were washed by being trodden in a vat by one man (Fig. 57),

Fig. 57 Fullers

Fig. 58 The fuller's assistant

while his next door neighbour did the rinsing. Fuller's earth would have been used instead of soap, and the clothes given careful drying and brushing before they were sent home again. Fig. 58 shows a fuller's assistant demonstrating how, by their process of cleaning, old clothes become as good as new. In St. Mark ix. 3, we read, 'And his raiment became shining, exceeding white as snow; so as no fuller on earth can white them.'

Vitruvius, in his tenth book, describes machines and engines, and it is obvious that the principle of the pulley was very well understood by the Romans. In a sepulchral relief of the Haterii, in the Lateran Museum, there is shown an excellent representation of a crane, and this we have used as the basis for our drawing (Fig. 59). The power is here man-power, applied by a treadmill. Our drawing shows how the weight of the slaves would turn the wheels and so wind on to a drum between them the ropes, which, passing through pulleys, are attached to the stone to be lifted.

The tomb dates from the end of the first century, and is not so much a work of art, as an advertisement in stone of the doings of the family; the inclusion of the crane rather points to the Haterii as having been successful building contractors, or, perhaps, crane makers.

Fig. 59 A crane

The crane would not have offered any great difficulty to the Roman in its making. Vitruvius describes a taximeter which, by an ingenious arrangement, dropped a pebble into a box for every mile of the journey, and a water-clock in which water dripping into a reservoir raised a float which turned the dial hands.

We may now pause to think how this trade and industry was carried on. Orders could not all have been given by word of mouth. A tile was found at Silchester which had scratched on it, FECIT TVBVL (um) CLEMENTINVS (Clementinus made this box-tile); another had SATIS (enough), and there were other graffiti, as these scratchings are called. These must be accepted as evidence that tile and brickmakers at Silchester knew how to write, and what is more, to do so in Latin. It is quite certain that the Romans did not import brickmakers, or that the Roman official made bricks for fun.

Another point to remember is that the Roman not only taught the Briton how to read and write, but he settled the form of our own letters. He took the alphabet of the Dorian Greeks, and gradually developed it into the form of the Trajan Column lettering. Inscriptions cut in stone have been found in Great Britain. Examples can be seen in the British Museum, and there is a very fine one on the front of a Roman tomb found in Westminster Abbey, which has been placed by the entrance to the Chapter House.

In writing we have the ordinary cursive, or handwriting, which was used by the Silchester brickmakers in their scratchings on the tiles, or by the authors for their manuscripts. It is believed that the shape of the letter in the Roman Cursive Script was influenced by the fact that much of it was scratched, either on metal,

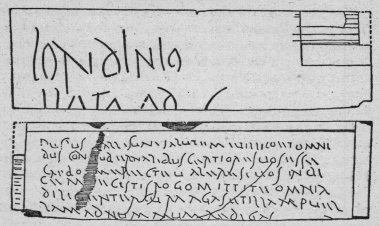

Fig. 60 Roman writing-tablet from London

or more commonly with a small iron pointed pen or
stylus on wax-covered wooden tablets. This made it
rather angular, and it was just as varied as handwriting is today. Fig. 60 shows a tablet found in
Walbrook – a river in the City of London. On the
outside it has LONDINIO, and on the inside the
message, which we will give in Latin, line by line, so
that you can read the Roman Cursive Script in the
illustration.

      Rufus callisuni salutem epillico et omni
—bus contubernalibus certiores vos esse
      Credo me recte valere si vos indi
—cem fecistis rogo mittite omnia
      diligenter cura agas ut illam puel
—lam ad nummum redigas.

This is believed to be the longest cursive inscription in
Britain, and this is how it reads in English.

Rufus, son of Callisunus Greeting to Epillicus and all his fellows. I believe you know I am very well. If you have made the list please send. Look after everything carefully. See that you turn that slave girl into cash ...

The message is unfinished but it is quite plainly a business message from Rufus to his manager – from one Roman-Briton perhaps on a trading journey to Verulamium or farther off to another Roman-Briton with the address on the outside LONDINIO.

However, the scribes, who wrote out official decrees, or made fair copies of poems or histories, used what is called Bookhand, which, as one would expect, is more beautiful than the cursive we have been looking at. At first they employed a form of writing which consisted of what we should call capitals. From this they developed into what is called Uncial writing, where the forms were rounded, and so more suitable to the pen.

Finally these scripts passed out of use, and with the decline of Roman Britain we find the primitive Britain creeping back into the writing. Silchester here provides us with another illustration, and this time it is one which speaks of the city in its decay. A stone was found there with an Ogham inscription cut on it. Ogham writing is a very primitive arrangement of dots and dashes, which seems to have been invented in Ireland, and the Silchester inscription is thought to date from about the fifth century. This, coupled with the burying of tools we noted on page 71, enables us to draw a picture of the deserted town falling into decay. Here, where the brickmakers at one time could scratch a Latin inscription on the wet clay of an unbaked tile, may have come, perhaps, a raiding

Scot, whose only means of writing was this very primitive method.

Having seen something of the trades and industries which grew up around the Romano-British house, we can now turn to the life lived therein, and see how the Roman fashioned his soul. In one of the houses at Silchester an interesting discovery was made of what is thought to have been the lararium or chapel.

Roman religion centred around the house; there was the Lar, or Lares, the spirit or spirits of the house, and a small bronze statuette (Fig. 61) found at Silchester, may have been one of these. Cicero, in a speech of 57 B.C., said:

> Is there anything more hallowed, is there anything more closely hedged about with every kind of sanctity than the home of each individual citizen? Therein he has his altars, his hearth, his household gods, his private worships, his rites and ceremonies.

Vesta was the spirit of the hearth, the Penates of the store closet, and Janus of the door. The father was the Paterfamilias, and acted as the priest, and his birthday was the festival of his Genius, or inspiring spirit.

There were gods of the city and the Vestal Virgins guarded the hearth fire of the State in their house by the Roman Forum, and here Janus dwelt in the Gate. Jupiter was the God of the sky, Juno of the Women, and Mars of War. The

Fig. 61 Bronze figure from Silchester

Fig. 62   Sacrifice

old Nature worship had developed, until almost everything had its spirit who must be propitiated by sacrifice.
The spirits became more tangible and the gods more
heroic, but they were feared and not loved. Instead of
the Christian belief that man is made in the image of
God, the old gods were made like man. What the
Roman wanted was the protection of the gods for the
safety of his family and the prosperity of his city. For
this he was prepared to pay a price, in the sacrifice
of the first-fruits of his crops, or by the life of his ox,
pig, and sheep; the god had the internal organs
dedicated to him on the altar, and the flesh was eaten.
What really counted was an elaborate ritual which
had to be followed with great particularity. Fig. 62 is
of a Roman sacrifice.

The Roman year was marked by a series of festivals
at varying seasons – the Saturnalia, at sowing, from
which many of our Christmas customs come; the
Robigalia, for the aversion of mildew; the Ambarvalia,
from which are derived Rogationtide processions
through the fields and the beating of bounds; and the
Consualia at the harvest; and there were many others.

Augustus effected a
great revival in Roman
religion. It was about this
time that we find the be-
ginnings of Caesar wor-
ship, which became gen-
eral, and was adopted for
political reasons. Here it
was not the man so much
as his Genius which was
worshipped.

Fig. 63 Mithras

As the Roman Empire
extended, many Oriental cults were grafted on to the
body of her religion, as those of Isis and Mithras. The
latter seems to have appealed especially to the soldiers,
and part of its ritual consisted of the novice being
initiated by grades including physical and mental or-
deals. Mithras was worshipped in underground
temples, of which there is a very interesting example in
the undermost of the three churches which form Ste.
Clemente in Rome. There are traces of a temple on
our Hadrian's Wall and another most interesting example of this curious underground religion has been
excavated at Walbrook in the City of London. The
underground temple was in a wonderfully complete
state of preservation, and the plan with seven pillars
representing the seven grades of Mithraism and a
sunken nave with raised side aisles in the Mithraic
manner could easily be seen by the thousands who
visited the site in the course of the excavation, attracted
by this unusual happening in the middle of the busy
London streets. Here too were found some splendid
marble statues, some of them wearing the cap of
Mithras like the figure in our illustration.

Apart from the soldiers' religions, which must have

been derived from all parts of the Empire we also find traces of little domestic British cults. Among the Roman-British farmers in the South of England Hercules seems to have been very popular. The hill-figure of the Cerne Abbas Giant, interpreted as Hercules with his club, is believed to date from Roman times. Hercules may also be connected with the rural temples in Norfolk and Suffolk. One of these at Wilton in Norfolk, was recently found by accident while a farmer was ploughing up a field. It contained a crown of five diadems (now in the British Museum) crudely cut out of sheet bronze and ornamented with single silver and bronze plaques stuck on with glue, and these have outline drawings hammered on them – a bearded face, a vase and two birds, a standing figure. This poorly made priest's 'regalia' looks like the costume for a children's play.

Alongside the Wilton 'Temple', which seems to have been a simple shed in a field, was another little hut containing a large collection of the little bronze safety pins of the sort which we have already illustrated. It seems in fact to have been a stall selling keepsakes to the visitors to this wayside shrine. At Wilton we have come a long way from the Imperial Roman religion, but perhaps it gives us a truer picture of what the ordinary people believed in Roman times. And perhaps we are nearer here to the origins of Christianity in these islands. For Christianity began amongst very humble people. ...

We must now return to our discussion of Roman ceremonial.

Fig. 64 shows the solemn clasping of hands (*dextrarum iunctio*) which formed an important part in the Roman wedding. The *pronuba* or matron friend of the bride, stands behind the bride and bridegroom, and the man

holds the marriage con-
tract in his left hand. After
this, prayers were offered
to the gods and sacrifice
made to Jupiter. The
bride, on the night before,
had put off her girl's
clothes and dedicated
them, with her toys, to the
Lares of her father's house.
On the wedding morn she
wore the *tunica recta* with a
woollen girdle, on her
head was a chaplet of
flowers, her veil was flame-
like, and her shoes were
saffron-coloured.

Fig. 64 Marriage

Our space will not permit us to write of the very
interesting ceremonies which were observed at the
birth of a Roman, or of all the festivals observed at
the various seasons of the year. So we must pass on
to the final stage of all – Death. We have in these
books paid considerable attention to the methods of
burial, and this must be done, because it is a detail in
the lives of man that is very indicative of the 'fashion
of the soul'.

As far back as the Mousterian Man of the Old
Stone Age, we have found men burying their dead
with varying ceremonial. In Roman times we find
that burials, which were not allowed within the city
walls, were placed instead along the roads leading
to the town. At Silchester, Roman interments have
been found at the side of the road leading to the
North Gate. In early Roman times, burial was carried
out by inhumation, that is by placing the body in a

coffin in a grave dug in the earth. This may be by
reason of their association with the Etruscans, who
are thought to have been of Mediterranean stock, and
so inclined to this method. Later, we find the Romans
cremating or burning their dead, the ashes being
disposed of in a variety of ways. Sometimes these
were placed in glass jars, protected by being placed
in leaden canisters; in other burials, pottery or
marble urns were used for the same purpose. These
were at times placed in graves, made in cist or boxlike
form, of red tiles about 2 feet square by 3 inches
thick. In these early cremations we find the old
custom of burying articles for use in the spirit world:
jugs, dishes, lamps, chairs, strigils, coins, mirrors,
brooches, have all been found in England. As Christianity spread, this changed, and the soul of the Christian
was not thought to need so many aids. Burial was
once again by means of inhumation in coffins of
wood, stone, or lead, the later ones lying east and
west with the head at the west. In modern times cre-
mation has again been introduced.

Funeral ceremonies were elaborate in Roman times,
and Fig. 65 shows the burial of an important person
of the time of Augustus. The dead body was laid out
on the funeral bed in the house, and dressed in the
toga. Torches burned at the corners of the bed, and
there were hired mourners; money was placed in the
mouth of the corpse, in Pagan times, to pay for the
spirit's journey. The procession was headed by musici-
ans, followed by the hired mourners, then came the
funeral bed in its litter, followed by the family. A
halt was made at the forum, and an oration delivered,
and the procession would go to the place of burning
outside the walls, where the body, being placed on a
pyre, was reduced to ashes, which were collected and

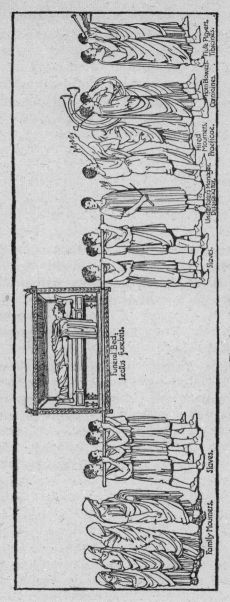

Fig. 65 A Roman funeral

Funeral Bed, Lectus funebris.

Family Mourners.

Slaves.

Slaves.

Undertaker's Manager, Dissignator.

Hired Mourners, Praeficae.

Horn-Blowers, Cornicines.

Flute Players, Tibicines.

placed in an urn. Afterwards there was a funeral feast.

Fig. 66 shows the tombstone of Gaius Saufeius, who served for twenty-two years in the 9th Legion, and dying at the age of forty, was buried at Lincoln. The tombstone is now in the British Museum, in the gallery on the ground floor, opposite the emperor he served. The extended inscription is:

C(AIO) SAVFEIO
C(AII) F(ILIO) FAB(IA) HER(ACLEA)
MILITI LEGIO(NIS) VIIII
ANNOR(VM) XXXX STIP(ENDIORVM) XXII
H(IC) S(ITVS) E(ST)

From which we learn that Saufeius came from Heraclea in Macedonia, and belonged to the Fabian tribe; but there may be descendants of him in Lincoln today who have forgotten their ancestry.

Funeral monuments, as that of the Haterii, whence came the crane (Fig. 59), afforded the Roman opportunities for the display of portrait busts. As we look at these today, it is easy to see that the portraits were speaking likenesses. It is interesting to note that with the advent of Christianity the dead were shown in attitudes of peaceful repose, until, with the coming of the Renaissance, they sit up and begin to take notice once more as in Roman times.

Fig. 66 A tombstone

4

THE ARMY, AND TRAVEL BY LAND AND SEA

IT would be well worth going to Rome to see only the Column erected by Trajan to commemorate his victories over the Dacians. Here, in a sculptured band which ascends the shaft in a slow spiral, we see the Roman soldier at work. And his work is not only fighting; very much he appears to have been the handy man of the Empire, able to build a city, as well as to destroy one. If we cannot go to Rome, there is a first-rate plaster model of the Column at the Victoria and Albert Museum, South Kensington.

During the first three centuries of the Empire, the army was divided into legions and auxiliaries – the former being the descendants of the early citizens and farmers who left the plough to fight, and auxiliaries recruited from subject peoples. A legion was known by a number, and equalled about 5000 heavy infantry and 120 riders for dispatches and scouting. It was commanded by a senator, nominated by the Emperor as commander-in-chief (*Legatus Augusti legionis*), 6 military tribunes of high social rank, 60 centurions who equalled majors and captains and were promoted from the ranks, and other inferior officers. Legionaries served with the colours for twenty years, and received a bounty and land on discharge.

The auxiliaries were divided into infantry cohorts of 500 to 1000 strong, and cavalry troops (*alæ*). They were commanded by Roman officers, prefects, or tribunes, and while their pay was less, their service was longer than the legionaries; they received Roman citizenship on discharge.

The Emperor's Praetorian Guard was stationed in Rome, but the remainder of the army was on the frontiers; here the legions stopped, and were not moved about. They were grouped with auxiliaries, and commanded by the Governor of the Province.

The battles of the Empire were won by the legionary (Fig. 67), who threw his javelin, and then rushed into close quarters and fought with his short sword (*gladius*), which was a cut-and-thrust weapon. The auxiliary cavalry operated on the wings, from which we get their name (*alæ*), and the Roman commanders do not appear to have wished to use them except in this way, thereby protecting the legionaries who delivered the main weight of the attack.

The tactics of this fighting at close quarters were to remain until the advent of the Martini-Henry rifle, issued to British troops in the 1870's which, by its longer range, removed the combatants from one another, and altered the whole strategy of fighting. The musket was not very much more effective, so far as range was concerned, than the longbow, and so long as it remained in use, the prob-

Fig. 67   A legionary

lem which confronted the soldier was the same as in Roman times – so to discipline your men that they would endure punishment until the psychological moment when the 'knock-out' could be administered.

The pilum of the legionary (Fig. 67) had an iron head fixed into a wooden shaft, and the weight of the iron head kept the javelin in a straight line when it was thrown. The killing range of the pilum was about thirty yards; compare this with the Tasmanian who could throw a wooden spear, nearly 12 feet long, and kill game at 40 to 50 yards. (See *Prehistoric Times*.) The notes on Fig. 67 will

Fig. 68   A centurion

explain the remaining equipment of the legionary. Fig. 69 shows the scale armour of bronze tinned that was sometimes worn instead of the *lorica segmentata*, and Fig. 70 the *caliga*, or sandal. Fig. 68 shows the equipment of the centurion. Fig. 71 is a belt buckle found at Newstead.

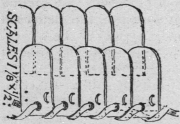

Fig. 69   Scale armour (*Lorica squamata*)

Fig. 70   Sandal (*caliga*)

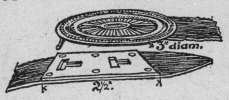

Fig. 71   A belt buckle

Fig. 72 shows an auxiliary, who wore only a leather jerkin, without body armour, an oval shield, and a longer sword, the *spatha* (Fig. 74). The auxiliaries who are shown on Trajan's Column wear the same dress whether fighting as cavalry or on foot. There were others as the slingers and stone-throwers (Fig. 73); the archer (Fig. 75); and the pioneer (Fig. 76), using his *dolabra*, a combination of pick and axe.

The soldiers were rewarded for acts of bravery. The officer has phalerae on his breast, and torques taken from the neck of his enemy hang from his shoulders. Crowns were given as a reward: the *corona triumphalis* of bay for the *triumphator*; of oak leaves for saving the life of a comrade; in the form of a ship's prow for the first to board an enemy ship; as a city wall for the man who stormed the walls; as a rampart for those who took camps; and of plain gold for pure bravery.

The ensigns were carried by men with a head-dress made of a lion's or leopard's skin. These served to mark the maniples, or units, of which the legion was composed, and enabled the commanders to direct the movement of their men.   Each legion

Fig. 72   An auxiliary

carried the eagle, and to lose it was to ensure disgrace.

The troops were accompanied by a medical corps. On Trajan's Column a wounded legionary is shown being assisted to a dressing-station, where an auxiliary is having his thigh bandaged in the modern way. At various points on the frontiers there were well-planned hospitals for sick troops.

Fig. 73 Slingers and stone throwers

The legionary was aided by effective artillery. Artillery is derived from a word which means to work with art, and doubtless the Roman did feel that his engines were works of art. They may have inherited the use of projectile-throwing engines from the Greeks,

Fig. 74
Swords

but these appear to have been in general use in the Near East after about 400 B.C. Vitruvius the architect, writing about the time of Augustus, gives descriptions and elaborate formulae for the construction of catapultae, scorpions, and balistae for throwing javelins and stones. Catapultae are shown on the sculptures of the Trajan Column, and there is another on the tombstone, in the Vatican, of *C. Vedennius Moderatus*, who was an *architectus armamentarii* in the Imperial arsenal at the end of the first century A.D. From these sources there have been various reconstructions of these old engines, and those of Sir Ralph Payne-Gallwey, shown in his book,

Fig. 75   An archer

are of great interest, because he has made actual working models.

The first consideration of the Roman engineer was to remove his engine outside the range of the bow. This raises the question of the length of the bowshot. With the English longbow, the very longest range was 440 yards; but the archer of the Trajan Column (Fig. 75) is shown armed with a bow of the Turkish pattern built up of horn and sinew, and there are accounts of shots of fabulous length with this. However that may be, the problem confronting the Roman engineer was not formidable, because it is obvious that the strength of the machine could very easily be made to exceed that of the man. Sir Ralph Payne-Gallwey succeeded in throwing a stone ball, 8 lb. in weight, from 450 to 500 yards, and he only depended on rope skeins for his power. The Greeks and Romans possessed the art of making these with hair and gut, but it was lost during the dark ages, and in mediaeval times the engineers depended on a counter-poised weight to throw the projectiles out of their trebuchets.

In classical times the power was obtained by torsion. Fig. 77 has been drawn from sculptures of the Trajan Column, and

Fig. 76   An axe (Dolabra)

Fig. 77   Roman field artillery. The catapulta

shows a catapult mounted on a small cart drawn by horses. The arms of the bow are composite, like the Turkish bow, and ends are fitted into the skeins of hair or gut. The ends of these skeins were passed through holes bored in the frame and then into large wooden washers. The skein was then secured by a pin through the centre, and was tightened by hand-spikes fitted into holes in the edge of the washer, and secured from springing back by catches, as shown. The skein was further tightened, when the bowstring was drawn back, by the winch at the end. This pulled back the carrier in which the javelin rested, and the bowstring being released, the heavy javelin flew off to come down into the besieged town. A variation of this engine for throwing stones was called the balista.

The onager in the same way depended for its power on a twisted skein, which in this case was horizontal. This skein was tightened in one way by hand-spikes as shown in Fig. 78, and in the other when the arm was pulled down by the windlass. This arm was built up to make it resist the shock of being stopped against the cross-piece of the frame. The stone ball, or rock, was placed in a leathern sling, and the trigger was a hook with an attachment by which it was pulled out of the ring on the arm. The stone ball, which was

Fig. 78　The onager

sent hurtling through the air, would have had sufficient force to crash through a roof.

The Romans also used the battering ram. In its simplest form, as shown on the Trajan Column, it consisted of a heavy beam which was carried by several men, and the point banged against the wall. After some few stones had been dislodged from the face, the rubble interior would not have presented so much difficulty to the breaching party.

Vitruvius gives descriptions of more elaborate forms, where the ram was suspended from the roof of a hut, made to run on wheels, and covered with raw hides, and as the machine moved slowly, it was called the tortoise of the ram.

Moveable towers were brought into use so that the besiegers could approach the walls of a beleaguered city and fire into it at more advantage than from on the ground; other moveable huts were contrived so that the ditches in front of the walls could be filled up, and the engineers, crossing on the causeway so formed, could undermine the walls.

The people of today who attempt reconstructions of these engines, are rather apt to provide their models with geared wheels enmeshed, the cogs of which could only have been cut on a machine; in our drawings we have suggested details which are much more home-made in character, and which the legionary could have made quite easily when he was far removed from his base; and we know, from the Trajan Column, that he was a very handy man.

Boys and girls will remember the dramatic part which catapults played in the destruction of Carthage. There was the mission of Cato to Carthage, in 157 B.C., from which he came back convinced that 'Delenda est Carthago'. Later, the Consuls, from their camp at Utica, demanded the surrender of all the Carthaginian weapons, and 200,000 sets of weapons, with 2000 catapults from the walls, were surrendered. Then came the final order, that Carthage was to be destroyed, and any new town that was built must be ten miles from the sea. It is one of the most tragic tales of history, how the Carthaginians, finding that they had been betrayed, seized on the scanty time which elapsed before the Romans started the siege, to re-arm themselves; how new weapons and missiles were made from the iron and lead of the buildings, and the women cut off their hair to make skeins for new catapults. The Carthaginians, behind their walls, maintained themselves against all the attempts of Scipio, until the last awful assault when the Romans cut their way in, from wall to wall, through the houses, to save the risks of fighting in the narrow streets. Then the last scene of all, when the wife of Hasdrubal, cursing her husband for his cowardly escape, killed her two sons, and perished with their bodies in the flames. Then the site of the town was obliterated by the plough and dedicated to the powers of the Underworld. It was all typical of the tough Roman spirit which would brook no rivals. If the drawings we have made of the war engines serve no other purpose than to invest the tale of Carthage with a new interest, and our readers with a determination to reconstruct on their own account, we shall be well repaid for our trouble.

We can now leave fighting and find out how the legionary lived. The soldiers were quartered in forts, around which towns grew up; the legions occupied the larger fortresses at some distance from the frontier, as at York, where they could march out to the support of the auxiliaries who were manning the Wall. The country round supplied the cattle and corn.

The greatest relic of all is Hadrian's Wall, built across the neck of England from the mouth of the Tyne to the widening of the Solway Firth. The whole length was a little more than 76 miles. Though much is left of the Wall, it does not stand its full height anywhere; this is estimated to have been about 15 feet – the breadth in most places is $7\frac{1}{2}$ feet. Along the top there must have been an embattled parapet where sentries could walk, though this walk could not have been wide enough to form a fighting-platform. In fact, archaeologists do not regard the Wall as a military work, in the sense of one made to repel large forces, but as a fortified boundary line, a customs' barrier, definitely separating the Roman from the non-Roman territory.

The sentries who watched the Wall were housed in square towers, called mile-castles, which are separated a Roman mile apart from each other. At intervals, too, there were turrets which are believed to have been signal stations. We know a good deal more about Roman signal stations than we did even a few years ago, as a number of foundations of these which had not been noticed in the old days have been discovered and excavated. On the English shore of the Solway they extended for some way beyond the end of the Wall. The means of signalling is not known; but there is evidence for the use in the Roman world of visual signals including flags, semaphores, torches, flares and beacons. At longer intervals were placed great forts in which the garrisons lived, which supplied men for duty at the mile-castles, and where forces were always ready to stand to arms in case of emergency.

Beyond the Wall was a ditch of defence. Another ditch, known as the *Vallum*,[1] ran at a short distance from the near (that is, the Roman) side of the Wall. This puzzled the antiquarians for a long while, for it is unusual to have a ditch on the *inner* side of a fortification. And the Vallum is not immediately next the Wall. Between them runs a military road to provide a means of communication and quick movement between points all along the line. But the mystery of the Vallum has now been cleared up. Its purpose was to prevent unauthorized civilians, not enemies, from approaching the military works of the wall. In places the line of the Wall passes over a tract of volcanic

[1] The word 'Vallum' means a mound and not a ditch. Originally there was a mound here on either side of the ditch. But in most places this has disappeared though the name is still attached to the ditch between the mounds.

basalt – the hardest rock we have. Yet, in spite of this, the Vallum has been arduously cleft out and faithfully follows its course. When, at the present day, you look down on the ground and see the very groove which the Romans themselves had scored to mark the farthest limit of their sway, it will be strange if you feel no thrill, no shock, no mental dizziness. For there is something so simple and positive about that mark that it seems to knit the past right up to us in a way that no ruin of masonry can. And then, while we may feel almost in touch with the times of Hadrian, the contrast of what was, and what is, strikes us from another angle, but still underlined by the Vallum.

For if, when we look at the Vallum, we are Roman-minded, we feel ourselves to be standing at the farthest edge of civilization, cut off from the mainland by a belt of sea – from that mainland on which, two thousand miles away, stands our metropolis, the chief city of the world. But, if we suddenly turn twentieth-century-minded, what a transformation of geography! Our metropolis is close at hand; it is on the same island; as the greatest city of the world it has taken the place of Rome. It is not on the fringe of an empire but at the heart of one. How much greater is this privilege of citizenship! Yet, we may ask ourselves, if that line had not been drawn in the rock from sea to sea, if the Romans had not founded their Londinium for us to build our London on, would it ever have been our turn to take so great and responsible a place in the history of the world?

In this same history, the Vallum is like one of those marks on the jamb of a door which records the annual growth of the youngsters of a family. By it we may see where Rome grew to her full stature. As a nation and an empire we have made our marks in other doorways. But the family is not yet grown-up. When it is, it will cease to mark individual statures. Perhaps the time is nearly at hand.

But there is another aspect to the Wall. In spite of its strength and the grandeur of its masonry and that of all the buildings connected with it, it is really a monument to failure and not success. When that pillar of triumph, whose foundations we have seen at Richborough, was raised there was no thought of a fortified partition in Britain. It was taken for granted that, although Agricola could not be left to consolidate the country he had marched over, his successor would complete that task. Even when it was found necessary to build Hadrian's Wall hopes of subduing the rest of the country were still confidently entertained. An important stage in this direction was the building of another wall between the Clyde and the Forth. This one, made of turf instead of stone, was constructed by Lollius Urbicus, who was Governor of Britain in the time of Antonius Pius. Under the name of the Antonine Wall, its ruins still remain. But it could not be held. It was too late. The Roman Empire was decaying. Instead, much work was continually put into the upkeep and repairs of Hadrian's Wall, which one must therefore regard as a monumental admission of defeat.

There were some sixteen large forts in connection with the Wall, and at more frequent intervals, smaller forts (mile-castles) and turrets.

As the Roman fort was just as carefully planned as the Roman town, it may be as well to describe it here. The fort followed the same lines as the camp. When the legion was on active service and camped for the night, it did so behind earthen walls of a regular

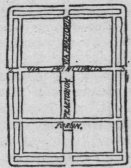

Fig. 79 Roman camp described by Hyginus

pattern. Polybius has left a description of the Republican Camp, and Hyginus of that of the Empire (Fig. 79). The praetorium, where the tent of the commander was pitched, formed the centre of the camp, and around it were grouped the quarters of staff and bodyguard. At the back was a forum where the soldiers could meet, and again behind this the quaestorium, or paymaster's office. The Roman forts were provided with granaries to hold sufficient corn for a year, so that they could withstand siege. Tribute was based on property and a corn tax which went to feed the army. The forts were provided as well with baths. The street in front of the praetorium was the Via Praetoria, and led to the Porta Praetoria, 1. The street which went across the camp was the Via Principalis, and led from the Porta Principalis Sinistra, 2, on one side, to the Porta Principalis Dextra, 3, on the other. The tents of the legionaries and their auxiliaries were pitched in the vacant spaces between these. When a fort had to be built, as at Newstead near Melrose, or on the Wall, the soldiers quite naturally built it in the form of the camp to which they were accustomed.

Wherever the Romans went they carried with them their love of the games, and here we would remind our readers that we shall obtain a very false perspective of history if we take our viewpoint from too modern an angle. We think of the doings of the Spanish Inquisition with horror, but Torquemada and Co. only adopted the usual methods of the secular courts of their time, the rack, pulley, and bucket of water, in their attempt to cure souls. In the same way we must remember that the *Meditations* of Marcus Aurelius, which have comforted many men since, were written by a man who must have attended the games. Originally these had formed part of religious ceremonies, and gladiators first appeared in the funeral games.

We have seen that there was an amphitheatre at Silchester (Fig. 6), and there was another at Dorchester (Fig. 80). Compared with the Colosseum, for example, these are simple constructions of earthen banks, but the displays given would have been much the same as those of Rome, though less elaborate.

Castor ware, which we have seen was an entirely British pottery, is sometimes decorated with gladiatorial combats. There is an ivory statuette of a gladiator in the British Museum, of the same type as shown in Fig. 81, and gladiators are shown in mosaic work at Bignor, Sussex. Beyond this we cannot go, and our readers if they like can people the amphitheatre we have shown. They can imagine the parade, and then the sham fight with blunt weapons, to be followed by the real thing. The gladiator (Fig. 81) might not have

Fig. 80 The amphitheatre at Dorchester

Fig. 81   A Samnite
gladiator

to fight against another armed in the same way, but could have been matched against the *retiarius*, armed with net, trident, and dagger. If the men held back they were thrashed into the fight with whips. There must have been wary feints, and lunges, and then a slip, when the net was cast, and the fallen man was hopeless in its entangling folds; but not perhaps quite hopeless, because if he had fought well, he could appeal to the spectators, and be granted reprieve if they waved their handkerchiefs; but if the thumbs were turned down then all that remained to the poor gladiator was one glance to where the bearers stood waiting with the bier for his dead body, before the dagger found a vulnerable spot, and his blood stained the sand. This may have happened at Silchester.

Fig. 82 has been drawn from the Ribchester helmet in the British Museum. This is made of thin bronze, and has a vizor modelled in the form of a face. An iron helmet of the same pattern was found at Newstead, and another of brass. It is thought that these helmets were used by the Celtic auxiliaries in their games.

Mr. Curle, in his book on Newstead, gives an account of the sports and exercises indulged in by the Roman cavalry in the time of Hadrian. From this we find that the vizor helmets were used by the men when taking part in a tournament, and were crested with yellow plumes; they carried gaily decorated shields and wore tunics, sometimes scarlet, or purple, and at others parti-coloured. Their horses were protected by frontlets and trappings from the showers of wooden spears which were discharged in the sham fights. Here is a pleasant picture of the legionaries grouped around the lists, into which ride these very gorgeous horsemen, to go through their evolutions; it was not all work in remote Newstead.

Having dealt with the Army and its bearing on British history, we can turn to the Navy, and just as the Roman generals did not rely on cavalry, so the Empire depended rather on the legionary than on sea-power. The Roman Navy seems to have been used more for the purposes of transport than as an effective fighting force.

When we come to the Roman ship, we find that there is not much more known about it than the Greek trireme; the writers were not sailors; the sculptors thought more of the design of their sculptures than the detail of the ships they were carving, and the sailors who did know, neither wrote, nor drew. Fig. 83, of a Roman galley, is based on those shown on Trajan's Column. The prow is carried up in forecastle fashion, and at the stern is a tilt. There are paintings at Pompeii showing galleys fitted with a mast and a square sail.

Fig. 84 is of a Roman merchant ship, and here

Fig. 82   Vizor helmet

Fig. 83   Roman galley

again we have gone to the Trajan Column sculptures, assisted by Professor Sottas' article in the *Mariner's Mirror*, on 'The Ship of St. Paul's Last Voyage'. This took place in A.D. 60, and is described by St. Luke in the 27th chapter of the Acts of the Apostles. This description is valuable, as showing the sizes, and general details, of the Roman ship at about the time when Britain was coming under the influence of Rome. We find that when the ship was caught in the easterly gale 'we had much work to come by the boat', which had been in tow, and had to be hoisted on board; by 'undergirding the ship' with ropes they added to its powers of resistance; they lightened the ship, 'and the third day we cast out with our own hands the tackling of the ship'. 'When the fourteenth night was come' the water shoaled rapidly from 20 to 15 fathoms, so that 'they cast four anchors out of the stern'.

The sailors were made of poor stuff, because they were 'about to flee out of the ship, when they had let down the boat into the sea, under colour as though they would have cast anchors out of the foreship'. We find that there were 'in all in the ship two hundred threescore and sixteen souls'.

Professor Sottas, in his article in the *Mariner's*

Fig. 84 A Roman merchant ship

Mirror, illustrates a model which he made of St. Paul's ship, based on the carving of a merchantman on a tomb at Pompeii, and another from Ostia, and these have many points of similarity with that of the ship on the Trajan Column. From these sources we find that the merchantman, or round ship, depended on its sails, and did not have oars like the galley; there was a tilt at the stern, with a gallery outside it, and another at the prow, with the crew's quarters behind in the forecastle. The mainsail and foresail were brailed up in a peculiar way, the sails were divided up into squares, with leather strips, having eyes at the intersections, and through these ropes were passed and the sail drawn up rather like a blind.

Now we come to one of the facts which, we think, illustrates what the Roman occupation meant to this country – the *pharos*, or lighthouse, which they built at Dover. The foundations still remain, and in Fig. 85 we show a galley which has made the cross-channel trip at night, and reached the land safely. During the Middle Ages, the lighting of the coasts was regarded as an act of piety, and a few lights were maintained on church towers, but it was not until well on in the nineteenth century that any real progress was made. Here, as in so many other ways, the Romans anticipated what was necessary in a civilized state.

If we leave our ship on the coast, we need roads to travel by on land, and this was an especial need for the Romans with their huge Empire to administer. By the roads were conveyed to and from Rome the official post and documents by which this administration was carried out. We are all of us far too ready to take things for granted; we walk on a Roman road, and are not thrilled; we may say, 'Well, after all, it is only a road', and we forget the travellers who through all the centuries, have hurried along its surface. It is interesting to speculate why a road should be in the position we find it. The answer, that it serves to connect two towns, may not contain the whole essence of the matter, because we can then ask why the towns have grown up in these places. There must be certain ways up and down a country, but these would not be very useful unless they connected areas where men could grow corn, or rear cattle, or find iron and coal with which to work.

Though there were 2000 years of farming in Britain before the Romans came, very little headway could have been made in clearing the land permanently for cultivation. We forget today what constant effort is needed to hold Nature in check, but a reminder can be seen at the Rothamstead Experimental Station,

Fig. 85   A Roman lighthouse

Harpenden, Hertfordshire. Here, some years ago, it was determined to leave untouched a piece of arable land and see what would happen. Gradually the weeds took possession, then bushes, and now large trees give the land the appearance of forests.

If we are motoring along a Roman road, it is noticeable that it goes in as straight a line as possible between the towns it connects, but if it is necessary to alter the direction this is done on high ground. This is thought to prove that the surveyors who laid out the roads in Roman times, did so by fires lighted on the hilltops. It would then be quite a simple matter to set out the intermediate points, sighting the flames by night or the smoke by day.

We may, in fact, think of the Roman roads as preparing us for our advancement in two ways. The most obvious of these is the ease which they enabled us to move from one part of the country to another. But this ease of locomotion brought another blessing with it. The roads, once established with their forts and strong-points, opened trade routes and founded trade-centres. Although the power of Rome declined, and her buildings fell into utter dilapidation and decay, the roads held out – in spite of neglect. They fostered the life-blood of the new civilization until the coming of the railways. When the railways were made, the centres of business and the market-towns were ready to make the most of the new form of transport, for *the roads had made the towns*. We, in our time, have seen the process reversed again. For now, since the coming of the motor, the towns make the roads.

But while many new arterial systems have come into use, from Telford's time to our own, the Roman roads are still the main thoroughfares both for touring-car and heavy vehicle. From Dover to London; from

London to Norwich, to Newcastle, to Chester; from
Chester to Carlisle; across the wild tops of the Pen-
nines the oil-driven rubbered wheel circulates our
civilization over the work of the Roman engineer.

Yet there is one great Roman road which has not,
and never has had, any continuous mission for com-
merce, that is the Fosse Way. It is the straightest
of the Roman roads and goes from Axminster, near
the south coast, to Lincoln, near the shore of the
North Sea, with no more than six miles out of the
same straight direction. Most of it is still to be traced,
and it is only used in places as a modern road. The
truth about it is that it was never intended to be used
as a commercial highway at all. It was made after
the first phase of the Conquest was completed – just
after the first half of the first century. It was made as a
military road, and something more than that. You
may compare it with the Vallum at Hadrian's Wall,
for it was constructed to indicate where the frontier
of the Roman Empire rested after the south-east of
England had been annexed and the first phase of
conquest completed.

The Fosse Way is also of great interest in showing
what an amazing grasp the Romans had of the life of
the land when they had only been here for three or
four years. They naturally had no maps; the country,
up to a considerable altitude, was covered with dense
forests; the inhabitants were hostile. Yet they mastered
a fact of our physical geography which many well-
educated people who have lived in England all their
lives are unaware of. They realized that there was a
natural division which parted England into two main
masses, and that it lay along the north fringe of the
Cotswold Hills, along the lower Severn Valley, and
then up towards the springs of the Avon. Here stands

the watershed. Beyond are the springs of the Soar; and the Soar Valley leads into the Trent Valley, which goes on in a direct line to the Humber and the salt water of the North Sea. The Fosse Way occupies the south side of this important division and, for the most part, does so in such a way as to command the country to the north-west.

The next powerful thrust was bent against Wales and no doubt went forward along the lines of what came, in later times, to be known as the Watling Street. This road, which is still in service for the whole of its length between Wroxeter (near Shrewsbury) and London, crosses the Fosse Way at the very point which we – having before us a physical map of Britain done in colours carefully and competently by H.M. Ordnance Survey – should have suggested ourselves. It crosses at the watershed, that small area which separates the waters of the basins of Severn and Trent. The place is called High Cross (*Venonæ* was the name of the Roman station), and is well marked by a peculiar Georgian milestone which takes the form of a small monument. From here the Watling Street takes a slight swerve to the west and ends its Roman course at Viroconium, now known as Wroxeter.

When they came to the construction of the roads, the Romans very properly used local materials: stone in a stone country, and flint and gravel where these were found. It is a mistake to think that the Roman road was always paved with stone, but one outstanding feature is that the road was almost invariably raised up on a causeway. The country was not so well drained as it is today, and so the causeway would have kept the road dry in the bottoms, yet the Romans would repeat it over the top of a chalk Down.

On our map (Fig. 1) we have given an outline of

what the principal authorities accept as the Roman road system.

Fig. 86 is of the milestone in the Roman Sculpture Gallery at the British Museum. The Roman mile was 1617 yards in length, and this stone was set up 8 miles from Kanovium (Caerhyn, near Conway). The Latin inscription is as follows:

```
IMP . CAES . TRAI
ANVS . HADRIANVS
AVG . P . M . TR . P
  . P . P . COS . III .
A . KANOVIO
  . M . P . VIII .
```

This they would have extended to IMPERATOR CÆSAR TRAIANVS HADRIANVS AVGVSTVS, PONTIFEX MAXIMVS, TRIBVNICIA POTESTATE. . . . PATER PATRIÆ, CONSVL III, A KANOVIO MILLIA PASSVVM VIII. The *British Museum Guide* points out that these are the titles of the Emperor Hadrian, and his third consulate dated from 119, but as the year of his tribunician power is uncertain, the inscription can only be dated between A.D. 119 and 138.

It must be remembered that our Roman roads were only a part of the system which radiated all over the Empire. Augustus set up a Golden Milestone in the forum at Rome, on which

Fig. 86 A Roman milestone

the distances to the principal cities of the Empire were given. He also set up a regular state post by which dispatches could be carried.

Fig. 87   A racing chariot

The Romans used various types of vehicles. There was the *lectica*, or litter, like the eighteenth-century sedan chair; the *ræda*, a four-wheeled waggon used when a number of people wanted to travel or luggage had to be carried. For faster travelling there were two-wheeled carts covered with a tilt and drawn by a mule.

Fig. 87 shows a pair-horse chariot which would have been used for racing or as a sporting conveyance. The bridle bit (Fig. 88) was found at Newstead, and Fig. 89 is of what is called a hipposandal, at the British Museum. Ordinary horse-shoes were known to the Romans, but smiths may have been few and far between. These hipposandals may have been used to tie on to the horses' hoofs as shoes when the farmer wanted to take his horses on to the hard roads, in much the same way as a horse wears shoes to prevent his feet cutting the turf when pulling a mowing machine.

As the history of Roman Britain depends largely on the Roman soldier, we can sketch it in very briefly here. The invasion of 43 was carried out by four legions and auxiliaries, in all probably about 40,000 men, and before the death of Claudius, the Romans had progressed as far west as Exeter, and Shrewsbury, and up to the Humber. From that time to the building of the Wall by Hadrian to define the northern frontier, was the period of conquest, the principal dates of which are noted in the Chronology.

The Romans penetrated into Scotland as early as the time of Agricola, but the north of Britain never passed out of the soldiers' hands, and few towns or villas were built to the north of York, or beyond Shrewsbury and Exeter. The second Legion was stationed at Caerleon, near

Fig. 88 A bridle bit from Newstead

Chepstow; the Twentieth at Chester, and the Ninth, and later the Sixth, at York. It is interesting to think of Britain as being the north-west Province of the Roman Empire, and needing as careful guarding as India in more recent times.

Britain must have owed a great deal to the wise government of Agricola, of whom we hear in the writings of his son-in-law Tacitus. It is probably during this period, A.D. 78–85, that Silchester, Bath, and Caerwent were commenced, and Latin began to be spoken, and the toga worn.

During the second century there were serious risings in the North, but the country on the whole was enjoying peace, and during the third century must have been very prosperous; after that began signs of the great upheaval which in the end was to overwhelm

Fig. 89 A hipposandal

Rome. The English became troublesome as early as
A.D. 300 when the Saxon shore was fortified against
them. This was done by a series of forts built round the
coast from the Wash to Portsmouth. The ruins of
many of these remain today, and one of the most
interesting is that at Porchester. Here the Roman walls
enclose a Norman church and castle keep which has
later Gothic additions. From the old ramparts one
looks out over the water of Portsmouth Harbour to
the Royal Dockyard due south. So here in this one
little spot is some 1100 years of architecture, and the
docks, with the forts on the hills behind, are a reminder
that watch and ward has been kept for over 1600 years.

Porchester is the best of the Saxon shore forts. It is
practically complete with its wall-walks and its
bastions, embracing the immense area of nine acres.
The next best are Richborough, Pevensey in Sussex,
and Burgh Castle at Yarmouth. There are relics at
Reculver (the far end of the sea channel between
Thanet and the mainland, of which Richborough was
the southern entrance), and at Lympne, on Romney
Marsh. Remains of the Roman fort at Dover are not so
certain, but the lighthouse already mentioned (page
110), still stands. Less known is the single example on
the west coast of the same type of fort as those of the
Saxon shore. This is to be seen at Holyhead. The
parish church stands within the enclosure.

At Richborough in Kent, one of the best known of
these Saxon shore forts, we have a complete picture as
to how things went from the beginning of the Roman
occupation to the end of it. In the old days, there was a
narrow sea passage between the mainland of Kent and
the Isle of Thanet. It was at the south end of this –
opening on to the Straits of Dover – that Richborough
was situated. The invading legions which came over

in the year 43 (page 116) landed here and threw up a double ditch and palisade to secure their first footing in our country. The actual remains of this can now be seen at Richborough since excavation has made it plain.

Near by, stands a mysterious cross-shaped mass of masonry which goes far down into the ground and is solid throughout. It is still something of a riddle, though perhaps more than half the answer has been guessed; for the fine detective work of the archaeologists has shown it to have been the foundation of an immense monument, the like of which was not raised in any other part of Britain by the Romans. That part of the riddle which remains unsolved relates to the purpose of this monument. But it is a fair guess that it was raised after the triumphs of Agricola to the conquest of the whole of Britain. At that time the major part of the work had been done, and it was thought the rest would be child's play. But Agricola was ordered to go and fight in another part of the Empire at the critical moment. And when matters were taken in hand again it was too late. Britain was never entirely conquered. The advanced wall, built beyond Hadrian's, between the inlets of Firth and Clyde, could not be held; and Scotland and Ireland remained till the end outside the boundary of the Roman Empire.

In the days when the monument was erected, Richborough was undefended. There seemed to be no need to defend it, for the English Channel was within the bounds of the Empire. But the name of Rome began to grow less awe-inspiring to the men who lived in the uncivilized 'outside' world, for political greed and struggles for power had weakened the spirit and the force of the nation. Macaulay writes as one who lived at that time when he says:

> Now Roman is to Roman
>   More hateful than a foe,
> And the Tribunes beard the high,
>   And the Fathers grind the low.
> As we wax hot in faction,
>   In battle we wax cold;
> Wherefore men fight not as they fought
>   In the brave days of old.

So the Barbarians grew bold, and took to the sea in raiding parties – Saxons from north of the Roman Empire's boundary in Germany and the men of the un-Romanized isle of Ireland, called at that early time the Scots. At Richborough, this time of fear, which was shortly after the year 250, is vividly illustrated by two rows of banks and ditches cast round the old landing-place (with the monument at its centre). It had been found necessary to defend the entrance to Britain. The defences were probably thought of as a temporary measure to stave off trouble until such time as Rome had reasserted herself, and come back into her old and proper glory. But the barbarian pirates, far from becoming quelled, grew more daring and more dangerous; and Rome, which had once relied on prestige for defending these open waters, had now come down to the more humiliating device of building local castles at the worst danger points. Thus, towards the end of the third century were built the immense stone walls of the fort at Richborough, which have remained to our own time, standing four-square round the works in earth and masonry, which mark the earlier stages of the Roman occupation of the country.

These walls are associated with a very dashing and picturesque character, the admiral Carausius, who made himself emperor by stealing his own fleet, and who struck such a number of penny pieces that they are among the commonest of the Roman coins which you may pick up anywhere in Britain. There is no room here to go into details of the adventures and career of Carausius, interesting as they are, but there is a significant thing to be noted about the building of the walls before we pass on from Richborough. Among the materials which have gone into their making are a number of pieces that can be said with certainty to have come from the structure which stood on the cross-shaped base and was, we guess, a monument to mark the triumph of the Roman arms in Britain. That fragments of this should be built into the walls raised nearly two and a half centuries after the time of Agricola, shows, first of all, that the monument must, even at that date, have been neglected and in ruins; and secondly, that it was no longer regarded as a thing to be proud of. Perhaps its presence was even felt to mock the Romans of that day and to commemorate failure rather than victory.

There were migrations of Celts, from Ireland to Caledonia, who were oddly enough called, not Irish, but Scotti. The Picts became troublesome about 343 and with the Scotti raided into England. Men began to bury their tools and treasures, as we have seen on page 70, and when hoards of coins are found, they are not, as a rule, dated later than 350–360. The most famous buried find is that of the Mildenhall Silver Treasure. This was found in Suffolk in 1946. The dishes and bowls had been carefully buried in the troubles at the end of the fourth century, and are still in beautiful condition after all this time. The treasure contains goblets, spoons, and bowls as well as beautiful platters and dishes. One still feels sad for the Romans who buried them so carefully in time of trouble and never returned to collect them.

It was about this time that the army was remodelled, and made more mobile, to meet the attacks of the Barbarians, with light troops, and more cavalry. The Governors were not trustworthy, and there were Dukes of Britain, Counts of Britain, and Counts of the Saxon shore, in case one alone should aspire to be Emperor.

Now we must not think of Britain all this time as having been occupied by a very large number of Romans who kept the British in subjection. As the latter settled down to Roman rule, the true Romans could not have been more than the official classes, and the skeleton of the army. We must imagine the more experienced of these being gradually recalled as the pressure on Rome increased. Many of the Britons were citizens of Rome, and looked on themselves as Romans; they did not stand on the cliffs at Dover, as the last boatload of Romans left, and cheer, thinking they had seen the last of their enemies. By this time they regarded themselves as Romans, and her enemies were theirs, and very terrible ones too.

The trouble started with a great stirring up of the peoples of the Central Asian plains. Driven perhaps by drought, the fierce and warlike Huns surged towards the Goths, whom they defeated. The vanquished moved across the Danube and Rhine, and, with the Huns behind them, were forced into the Roman Empire. Rome was captured and sacked in 410, and the movement was not stopped until Attila, the King of the Huns, was defeated at Châlons in 451. By this time the elaborate organization of the Empire had broken down, and Europe had entered into the Dark Ages.

Here in Britain we can imagine the Britons holding their own as best they could against their enemies, but being gradually forced into the west, where they joined up with the Celts, and settled down in a primitive environment. Those who did not fly would have been killed, or sold into slavery. The Jutes, the Angles, and Saxons must have come up to a deserted Silchester, and have gaped at its wonders, as something entirely outside the range of their understanding. Britain and Europe were to wait for a thousand years before the ideas which Silchester expressed again became the thought of the day.

INDEX

The numerals in bold type refer to the figure-numbers of the illustrations